Instructional Materials
for
Bilingual Vocational Education

EVALUATION, MODIFICATION, AND DEVELOPMENT

Joan E. Friedenberg and Curtis H. Bradley

 THE CENTER FOR APPLIED LINGUISTICS

Instructional Materials
for
Bilingual Vocational Education

EVALUATION, MODIFICATION, AND DEVELOPMENT

HBJ HARCOURT BRACE JOVANOVICH, INC.

Orlando • San Diego • New York
Toronto • London • Sydney • Tokyo

Printed in the United States of America

Typographical design: Harry Rinehart
Cover art: Fitzgerald & Swaim, Inc.

ISBN 0-15-599300-3

Contents

Introduction

Instructional Materials for Bilingual Vocational Education was developed in response to the growing national need to provide relevant vocational instructional materials to limited-English-proficient persons who are receiving vocational instruction or on-the-job training. Thus, its main purpose is to assist vocational instructors and job trainers of LEP students or workers to locate resources and to evaluate, adapt, and develop their own training materials.

As an in-service tool, the book can be used by secondary and adult vocational instructors, aides, counselors, placement specialists, job developers, administrators, workshop clinicians, consultants, curriculum specialists, materials developers, and any other personnel involved with bilingual education or vocational education programs at the secondary and adult levels; industrial training both here and abroad; or refugee assistance programs.

As a pre-service tool, the book is applicable to graduate or undergraduate courses in Bilingual Education, Instructional Materials for Vocational Education, Vocational Special Needs Education, Adult Education, and Bilingual Vocational Education.

The book is divided into six chapters. The first describes nine areas of national resources for obtaining information about and materials for bilingual vocational instruction. Chapter Two describes how to utilize one's local community as a resource.

The third chapter presents guidelines for evaluating and modifying English vocational materials for use with limited English-proficient students and the fourth presents guidelines for evaluating bilingual and non-English vocational training materials.

Chapter Five describes the process of developing instruction sheets for bilingual vocational instruction and chapter Six describes the process of developing individualized learning packages for LEP vocational students. Following the final chapter are numerous appendices containing a good deal of information about instructional resources for anyone working with LEP adults and secondary students.

For a general orientation to the field of Bilingual Vocational Education, refer to Bradley and Friedenberg, *Foundations and Strategies for Bilingual Vocational Education*, Washington, D.C.: Center for Applied Linguistics, 1982.

CHAPTER 1

National Resources
for Bilingual Vocational Education

There are a number of sources which a vocational instructor of limited-English-proficient (LEP) students can explore to find information about and/or materials for bilingual vocational instruction. Many of these materials are available free of charge or on a cost-recovery basis; others are generally available for examination before purchasing. You should make an effort to become familiar with these sources, since they can be time-saving and enlightening, and most important, they exist to serve you.

THE THREE C'S: CENTERS,
CLEARINGHOUSES, AND CURRICULUM LABS

These are the best sources for materials and information available free or on a cost-recovery basis. Those currently in existence which could provide resources of interest to the vocational instructor of LEP students are described below.

1. *Clearinghouse for Adult, Career and Vocational Education,* Ohio State University, 1960 Kenny Road, Columbus, OH 43210.

This is one of the 16 Educational Resources Information Center (ERIC) Clearinghouses. Its purpose is to identify, select, process, and disseminate information on adult and continuing education, career education—preschool through adult—vocational and technical education, and education and work.

A major reference provided by this Clearinghouse is *Resources in Vocational Education* [formerly *Abstracts of Research and Related Materials (ARM) and Abstracts of Instructional Materials (AIM)*], which includes abstracts of such materials as research reports, curriculum guides, program descriptions, and state-of-the-art papers. *RVE* is published monthly and is available in many libraries. Additionally, copies of the original materials reported in *RVE* are available in hundreds of locations nationally. A listing of ERIC facilities around the country and a brochure describing how to use the ERIC system are available at no charge upon request.

> 2. *National Clearinghouse for Bilingual Education (NCBE),* 1555 Wilson Boulevard, Suite 605, Rosslyn, VA 22209; (800) 336-4560 or (703) 522-0710.

This center was founded in 1977 by the National Institute of Education and the Office of Bilingual Education and Minority Languages Affairs of the U.S. Department of Education. Its aims are to provide a reference and referral service (via its toll-free hot line); conduct computer searches; publish a monthly newsletter (*Forum*); publish books, articles, and manuals; and prepare information packets. These services are available free or on a cost-recovery basis to anyone seeking information about bilingual education, including bilingual vocational education.

> 3. *National Center for Research in Vocational Education,* Ohio State University, 1960 Kenny Road, Columbus, OH 43210.

The National Center for Research in Vocational Education's mission is to increase the ability of diverse agencies, institutions, and organizations to solve educational problems relating to individual career planning, preparation, and progression. The Center conducts numerous studies, publishes useful professional literature (guides, reports, and instructional and workshop materials), and conducts special training programs. In addition, it publishes the *Vocational Educator* and *Centergram* to announce products and services available through the center.

> 4. *Center for Applied Linguistics* (CAL), 3520 Prospect Street, N.W., Washington, D.C. 20007.

The Center for Applied Linguistics is a private, non-profit organization involved in the study of language and its application to educational, cultural, and social concerns. CAL conducts research, carries out technical assistance activities, and publishes materials in collaboration with Harcourt Brace Jovanovich International. CAL has been a leader in the area of refugee assistance and education. It also houses the Refugee Service Center (RSC) and the ERIC Clearinghouse for Languages and Linguistics. CAL presently carries materials related to vocational English as a second language and bilingual vocational education, which are distributed worldwide by HBJ.

5. *Evaluation, Dissemination, and Assessment Centers* (EDAC), 49 Washington Avenue, Cambridge, MA 02140.

   3700 Ross Avenue, Box 103, Dallas, TX 75204

   California State University, 5151 State University Drive, Los Angeles, CA 90032

The major function of these centers is to develop and disseminate educational materials—books, audio-visual aids, visual aids, etc.—in a number of languages. Although most publications are aimed at students on the K–12 level, there are career awareness materials which could be useful for both secondary and adult students. The center provides materials in the following languages: Cape Verdean, Chinese, English, French, Greek, Haitian Creole, Italian, Japanese, Korean, Portuguese, Spanish, and Vietnamese.

CURRICULUM CENTERS/LABS

Individual states have curriculum centers or laboratories that make available a wide range of curriculum materials and related implementation assistance. Services provided to vocational educators vary from state to state and may include:

- producing and disseminating Vocational Technical Education Consortium of States (V-TECS) catalogs;
- developing and disseminating inservice training packages;
- developing curriculum materials, such as guides, manuals, and modules;
- performing research;
- providing technical assistance;

- acquiring, classifying, and storing curriculum materials for retrieval in response to requests;
- researching and adapting materials developed by other states and organizations;
- providing occupational analyses and performance objectives on a cost-recovery basis;
- providing free film loans; and
- serving as a computerized resource center.

The National network for Curriculum Coordination in Vocational-Technical Education is a federally-funded service organization which provides a system for sharing vocational curriculum products and information on a regional basis. The National Network operates through six Curriculum Coordination Centers. (See Appendix A for a description of each of the state centers and a listing of the six National Curriculum Coordination Centers.)

OTHER PROGRAMS

Existing programs are one of your best sources of materials and information. Since bilingual vocational instruction is such a new idea, most programs have had to develop their own bilingual training materials. Many of them are willing to share these materials with interested outsiders, particularly because of the feedback such sharing often brings. We urge you to help in this effort by writing a formal letter expressing your appreciation for these materials and including a description of how the materials were specifically helpful to you and your program. You can find existing programs by contacting the U.S. Department of Education and the various departments of education on the state level.

PROFESSIONAL ASSOCIATIONS, JOURNALS, AND MEETINGS

Professional associations and their related journals and meetings are excellent sources for information and personal contacts. The annual meetings which associations sponsor for their membership are particularly valuable as a source for instructional materials.

In addition to a multitude of formal and informal presentations on a wide range of topics, professionals attending these conferences find large numbers of commercial publishers and manufacturers displaying and demonstrating their latest products.

Although the five associations described below serve either a "bilingual" or "vocational" audience, each has special interest sections for those educators specifically interested in bilingual vocational instruction. Each association charges dues. Most also have local, state, or regional chapters.

1. *American Vocational Association (AVA)*, 2020 N. 14th Street, Arlington, VA 22201.

    Journal: *Voc Ed* (published 10 times per year).
    Membership: For vocational teachers, administrators, supervisors, teacher educators, researchers, guidance counselors, and others concerned with vocational education at the secondary, post-secondary, and adult levels.
    National convention: Each December.

2. *National Association for Bilingual Education (NABE)*, Room 405, 1201 16th St., N.W., Washington, D.C. 20036.

    Journal: *NABE Journal.*
    Membership: For teachers, administrators, students, paraprofessionals, parents, or college instructors interested in bilingual education. There is a Vocational Education Special Interest Group.
    National convention: Each Spring.

3. *National Association of Vocational Education Special Needs Personnel* (NAVESNP, a section of the AVA). Write to the American Vocational Association for the addresses of current officers.

    Journal: *Journal for Vocational Special Needs Education.*
    Membership: For professionals employed in programs or services related to vocational education special needs (i.e. disadvantaged, learning disabled, hearing impaired, LEP, etc.).
    National convention: Conducts annual presentations and meetings each year as part of the AVA convention.

4. *Teachers of English to Speakers of Other Languages (TESOL).* James E. Alatis, Executive Director. D.C. Transit Building, 2nd Floor, Georgetown University, Washington, D.C. 20057.

   Journal: *TESOL Quarterly.*
   Membership: For those concerned with the teaching of English as a second or foreign language and of Standard English as a second dialect. There is an Adult Education Interest Section.
   National convention: Each March.

5. *Vocational Instructional Materials Section* (VIMS, a section of the AVA). Write to the American Vocational Association for the addresses of current officers.

   Membership: For educators engaged or interested in the preparation and dissemination of instructional materials.
   National convention: Conducts an annual membership meeting each year as part of the AVA convention.

FUNDING SOURCES

The conscientious vocational instructor of LEP students might find it useful to advise her or his supervisor of the availability of grants to initiate or improve bilingual vocational training. A note of caution should be injected here. Although it is certainly worthwhile for vocational instructors or counselors to be aware of these sources and to make their colleagues and supervisors aware of them, care must be taken to go through the proper administrative procedures for obtaining outside funds. The interested principal or director is urged to first communicate with the district superintendant's staff to obtain advice on and assistance for preparing a grant proposal.

The best sources for information on funding are listed below. Be sure to obtain the most recent address.

1. Office of Bilingual Education and Minority Languages Affairs (OBEMLA)
   U.S. Department of Education
   Washington, D.C. 20202

2. Office of Vocational and Adult Education
   U.S. Department of Education
   Washington, D.C. 20202

3. Many state departments of education are also beginning to provide some funds for bilingual vocational education. Program area supervisors can provide names and addresses of the appropriate individuals to contact.

COMMERCIAL PUBLISHERS

Many commercial publishers of vocational training materials are now beginning to make their materials available in more than one language. Distributors of training materials are now also making foreign vocational training materials available in the U.S. (A list of publishers and distributors of bilingual and non-English vocational materials is provided in Chapter 5 of this handbook.)

MANUFACTURERS AND DISTRIBUTORS

Items such as the manufacturer's specifications, installation guides, owner's manuals, and product utilization reports and instructions are also useful as instructional resources in vocational education. Therefore, most manufacturers and/or distributors are potential sources of instructional resources. A growing number of manufacturers and distributors are supplying such material in more than one language.

An experienced instructor's knowledge of an occupational area is the most immediate source of information regarding manufacturers who provide useful literature. Exhibits at state, regional, and national conferences are equally productive sources. Even more readily available are trade or professional journals such as *School Shop* that contain advertisements and product information listings designed exclusively to offer such material to interested professionals.

MILITARY CURRICULUM MATERIALS

The military conducts extensive occupational training programs for which they develop curriculum materials. These materials are based upon extensive task analyses and include complete performance objectives. All of these materials have been field-tested, evaluated, and revised, and most of the recent ones reflect the present emphases on individualized and programmed instruction, as well as innovative teaching strategies.

A special project of the National Center for Research in Vocational Education acquires, screens, and modifies military curriculum materials for civilian vocational technical education use. The selected materials are available through the Educational Resources Information Center (ERIC) and through curriculum coordination centers participating in the project.

FEDERAL AGENCIES

A number of federal agencies have developed literature that has direct application to vocational education. A list of vocational instructional materials available from federal agencies can be obtained by writing to:

> Ms. Muriel Shay Tapman
> National Projects Branch, D.O.E.
> ROB #3, Room 5028
> 7th & D Streets, SW
> Washington, D.C., 20202

Other materials that might also be useful, but are not specifically written for student use, are disseminated through the U.S. Government Printing Office. A catalog of publications can be obtained at the local library or by writing to:

> Superintendent of Documents, U.S. Government Printing Office, Washington, D.C. 20402

STATE AGENCIES

Within the department of education of each state there are teams of specialists concerned with vocational education, special education, and bilingual education. A few concerned states have bilingual vocational education specialists. There is also a Research Coordinating Unit with a staff of specialists concerned with all aspects of vocational education. All of these specialists and others within your state are available to help you and your program. Contact should be made through your school administration.

PRACTICE

1. Name five places you could write to for free information about bilingual vocational education.

2. Name two places you could write to for information about funding a bilingual vocational training program.

3. Where is the nearest curriculum laboratory to your school?

4. Name two professional organizations which could help you meet others interested in bilingual vocational education.

CHAPTER 2

Four Steps to Utilizing Community Resources: Deciding, Digging, Doping, and Doing

Every school district has a multitude of human resources officially available to help enrich a bilingual vocational education program. Program area supervisors, curriculum specialists, content consultants, and a variety of other professionals are employed to provide specific assistance to teachers. In addition, there are human resources that are "unofficially" available to every teacher. These include experienced teachers, custodians, and the clerical staff, who can also provide a number of informal but useful services.

There is also a wide range of resources outside of the formal and informal organization of the school district that is available to the interested instructor. Highly trained and competent individuals from business, industry, governmental and social service agencies, professional, and fraternal organizations are just a sampling of the kinds of resources available in any community. These community resources can support, strengthen, and enrich any vocational-technical education program and are readily available to the enterprising teacher or administrator. All that is required is to follow the four steps to utilizing community resources: Deciding, Digging, Doping, and Doing.

DECIDING

The first step toward effectively utilizing community resources is to decide what the appropriate community resources could do for the program. Stated differently, the first step is to determine your objective. Why do you want to use community resources? How can you use these resources?

Community resources can be used to meet broad needs of bilingual vocational-technical education programs. Some of these needs include student recruitment, selection, and placement; providing for student recognition; updating or modifying instruction; improving public relations; or even helping make appropriate social services more readily available to students (and staff).

After identifying some broad areas where community resources could help the program, it is useful to identify specific tasks that can be accomplished through utilization of community resources. Brainstorming is an effective method for this. Interested educators form a "think tank" and list as many specific tasks as possible that could be done to help the program under each of the broad categories of need that have been selected for strengthening. The normal rules of brainstorming apply (i.e. recognizing that the more ideas generated, the better the end product; not criticizing any idea; and encouraging building on the ideas of others). The next step is to "dig out" the community resources.

DIGGING

This step simply involves gathering information. Educators begin looking at the community, talking to knowledgeable individuals, and building lists.

A good place to begin is the reference desk of the library. Most libraries will have a commercially prepared *State Industries Guide*, a *Chamber of Commerce Directory of Industries*, the *Encyclopedia of Associations*, directories of national corporations with local officers, a directory of industrial parks, and similar publications. Therefore, it is relatively easy to develop a list of the names, addresses, principal officers, and other information about major companies located in the area. The United Way (or United Fund) will readily supply similar information about social service agencies. School districts also often have comprehensive directories of community resources.

The yellow pages section of the telephone directory is another excellent source of information. Local businesses are quickly found under the appropriate headings. Business and trade organizations, chambers of commerce, fraternal organizations, fraternities and sororities, labor organizations, political organizations, professional organizations, social service organizations, veterans' and military organizations, youth organizations, and senior citizens' organizations each have their own heading in the yellow pages, and each is a potential resource for the interested vocational educator. We were astonished, for example, to learn that there are no less than 85 newspapers listed in the yellow pages of our telephone directory.

Local and state governments generally have a citizen's information service that also can supply valuable information about community resources. Other educators are another excellent source of information about the community: Guidance counselors, placement specialists, teachers, and administrators each have valuable knowledge that can be tapped. Many school districts and universities have bilingual education or English as a second language programs which can provide valuable assistance. In addition, community ethnic groups often form cultural and/or political associations which can be of service to your program.

Thus, gathering information is simply a matter of looking, talking, and building lists. You will be surprised when you see the number of resources that are available. The next step is to determine what to do with these resources.

DOPING

This step involves answering the question, "Now that you know what you have, how can you use it?" After developing the comprehensive list of community resources, it becomes apparent that for almost every need there exists a group that can help meet it. The only limitation appears to be the educator's imagination and initiative in securing assistance.

It must be understood that projects are more popular if they are of short duration or at least have a terminal point. They also appeal to an organization if they help the organization achieve its goals or are related to its objectives or interests. For example, Toastmasters' clubs prefer projects where members actually perform speaking tasks. Veterans' groups enthusiastically support citizenship-oriented projects. Lions clubs like work with the blind or vision-saving projects. The stated purpose and major interests of social service agencies are in the printed literature each agency makes available to the public.

It must also be understood that the potential contribution of each community resource is not necessarily limited to its officially stated purpose. Large corporations are a case in point. With certain corporations the direct reliance upon a given vocational-technical education program is clear-cut. In these cases, supporting the educational program that supplies prospective employees can be viewed as enlightened self-interest. However, even in cases where the direct relationship between a corporation and a vocational program is not evident, or is even non-existent, the growing concept of corporate social responsibility can be a major influence. The increased awareness of corporate responsibility to society makes most major businesses and industries prime prospects for helping support, strengthen, and enrich vocational-technical education programs.

The "doping" step of utilizing community resources is the process of fitting the program needs to the group best suited to help. Group interest can be matched to program needs if we know the basic purpose, function, and interests of the group. When this match has been made, a request for support is developed that is tailor-made for the group.

DOING

The "doing" step is just plain asking for help. *How* this step is carried out is probably the most crucial part of the entire process. It is essential that the request for support be specific and thorough. Groups and individuals will support projects that are significant and specific in terms of need, time, cost, and extent of involvement.

In some instances the presentation is made by an enthusiastic educator or advisory committee member. However, it is not unusual to recruit a small group of influential members of the community whose exclusive purpose is to sell the organization on adopting the project. Group members must, of course, be genuinely committed to and well versed in the program needs they will present. After preparing and rehearsing their presentation, they schedule an appointment and make the presentation as a group. In most cases the request is made to the organization's officers, executive group, or directors, or to a specific committee. In some cases, this is followed by a presentation at a regular meeting of the entire group. *In all cases, a specific and thorough presentation is essential.*

It is impossible to discuss the topic of utilizing community resources without emphasizing that recognition is also an essential ingredient. Gratitude for a task well done can be expressed in the form of a letter or certificate of appreciation, articles in company magazines or bulletins, hand-lettered scrolls, or resolutions of advisory committees. There are many ways to say thank you, and any job well done deserves the best.

PRACTICE

1. Identify two ways in which community resources might enrich your bilingual vocational program.

   _____

   _____

2. Identify three possible resources from your community.

   _____

   _____

   _____

3. Explain how each of the above resources could contribute to your program.

   _____

   _____

   _____

4. Describe the steps you would take to recruit them.

   _____

   _____

   _____

CHAPTER 3

Evaluating and Modifying
English Vocational Materials
for Bilingual Vocational Instruction

This chapter begins with three assumptions:

- Before educators can adequately evaluate and modify materials, they must have a thorough knowledge of the students who will use the materials. This entails finding answers to the following questions.
    a. How well can they read in English?
    b. Can they read in their native language?
    c. How much technical knowledge of the field do they have?
    d. How well do they understand spoken English?
    e. How well do they express themselves in spoken English?
    f. How well can they write in English?
    g. What kind of influence can the students' culture have on their attitudes and approaches to learning?
    h. How much formal education have they had?
- The major goal of the instructional program should be to prepare students to successfully obtain and keep employment in the U.S. Although there are certainly occupations and geographic areas in the U.S. where bilingualism on the job is desirable and necessary, students must be able to function on the job in English. The degree to which English must be learned (e.g., oral, written, formal written, etc.) depends upon the particular occupation.
- Limited-English-proficient vocational students have a moral and legal right to instructional materials which they can both understand and benefit from.

EVALUATING MATERIALS

Although several excellent and lengthy checklists have been developed for evaluating vocational instructional materials, these complex instruments are more appropriate for administrators and curriculum committees, as they are in a position to decide whether certain materials should be purchased. Very often, however, vocational instructors find themselves in situations where they are provided with materials with which they must "make do." Thus their task is not to decide *whether* certain materials should be ordered, but *how* to make the most of materials they already have. In order to do so effectively, they need quick and efficient ways to evaluate the strong and weak characteristics of the materials and to modify the weak parts. Instructors should take on this evaluative role because they are most familiar with the needs of the users of the materials, i.e., their students.

For instructors with LEP students, evaluation should take place in four areas: (1) language, (2) bias, (3) content, and (4) physical appearance.

Language: Can the students understand the language of the text?

1. Does the text avoid terminology that is more complex than it should be for the job?
2. Is the terminology complex enough for the job?
3. Does the text provide clear explanations of terms?
4. Is the text free of slang, archaic, or otherwise uncommon words?
5. Are the sentences in the text simple and not too long?

Biases: Are there cultural and sex biases which may affect comprehension of the text or student attitudes towards the text?

1. Do illustrations of people have multi-ethnic representation?
2. Do illustrations of people include more or less equal distributions of female and male figures at all occupations and levels?
3. Is the language of the text free of cultural and sex-role stereotyping? For example, does the text use she/her as

well as he/him? Does it use women's names as well as men's in its examples?

4. Do the learning activities represent the learning styles of students from various cultural backgrounds (application and rote learning, competition and cooperation, multiple choice and free response, oral and written, etc.)?

Content: Is the content of the text appropriate?

1. Is the content of the text consistent with the course objectives?
2. Is the information in the text accurate and up-to-date?
3. Does the organization of the text follow a logical sequence?
4. Is the text free of unnecessary detail?
5. Are enough examples provided?
6. Are there enough clear illustrations and diagrams which can help students who have limited proficiency in English?
7. Are the learning activities useful and job-oriented?
8. Are there enough activities which students can do on their own?
9. Are there enough activities which provide students with opportunities to work cooperatively?

Physical Appearance: Does the physical appearance of the text affect its readability?

1. Are the words on a page easy to see (i.e., large enough, dark enough, enough spacing, etc.)?
2. Are headings, key points, and key terms especially easy to spot?

MODIFYING MATERIALS

Identifying the undesirable characteristics of vocational materials is only half the job of providing multicultural student populations with appropriate instructional materials. The conscientious instructor must also seek ways to change these characteristics. Fortunately, this task is not as difficult as might be supposed, and its benefits clearly outweigh the time required to perform it.

By modifying vocational materials, instructors:

- learn to be sensitive to students' special needs,
- learn how to conform to the desires of the school administration while also being true to their own desires as individuals,
- have an easier job in the classroom or lab, since understandable materials can do a good deal of explaining on their own, and
- contribute to the training and ultimate employment of those who are often un- or underemployed.

Language Modifications

1. If students are severely limited-English-proficient, *parts* of the text, i.e., headings, key points, definitions of important terms, summaries, and safety precautions, etc., should be translated into the students' native language. Translations can be taped into the text over the English, placed on margin tabs,* or provided on a supplementary instruction sheet (see Chapter 6). The instructor can acquire translation assistance from advanced bilingual students or from bilingual colleagues and community members.

2. If the text contains overly-complex, slang, or archaic terms, these should be replaced with more appropriate ones (stripped in on top of old ones, in the margins, on margin tabs, or on a supplementary instruction sheet).

3. If the terminology is too simple or childish, the students should be given a list of more appropriate terms on a supplementary information sheet.

4. If the text contains appropriate terms but does not adequately explain their meanings, definitions should be provided on margin tabs or on a supplementary information sheet.

5. If the sentence structure of the text seems too complex, simple and concise summaries of each important part should be provided on margin tabs or on an information sheet. The instructor may simply wish to "guide" the students through the text with the assistance of an assignment sheet (see Chapter 6).

---

* The idea of using margin tabs came from Susan B. Adams, *Serving Students with Limited English Proficiency: A Guide for Kentucky Vocational Educators* (Bowling Green, KY: Western Kentucky University, 1981), p.123.

Modifications to Eliminate Bias

1. If illustrations represent persons from only one ethnic group or if they over-represent one sex, more appropriate illustrations can be placed over the old ones or supplementary illustrations can be shown to the students while the instructor makes the point that the text's illustrations contained culture and/or sex biases. (See Appendix C.)

2. If the language of the text contains cultural or sex-role stereotyping, new expressions can be placed on top of the old ones or in the margins. The instructor should bring the bias to the students' attention. Instructors who understand that vocational education involves more than teaching psychomotor skills may even wish to afford students the opportunity to make their own suggestions for eliminating the biased language. (See Appendix C.)

3. If the learning activities presented in the text seem to favor the learning styles of students from the dominant culture only, the instructor should seek suggestions for alternative activities from colleagues, advanced bilingual students, community members, or experts in multicultural education. When alternative activities have been identified, they can be added to the text on margin tabs or on appropriate Supplementary Assignment Sheets, Job Sheets, Experiment Sheets, and Operation Sheets (See Chapter 6).

Content Modifications

1. If the text content does not coincide exactly with the course objectives, only those parts which do fit should be used. The rest of the content should be provided on supplementary instruction sheets if or when it is needed.

2. If some of the information in the text is not accurate or up-to-date, the corrected information can be placed over the old information or on a margin tab. If a good deal of information must be added, an appropriate instruction sheet should be used.

3. If the text does not seem to follow a logical sequence, the units or sections should be re-sequenced appropriately. Provide the new sequence on a separate sheet (for re-sequencing the units of an entire text) or on a margin tab (for re-sequencing the sections within one unit).

4. If the text contains unnecessary detail, a concise summary of the key points should be provided on a margin tab or information sheet. The instructor may prefer to "guide" the students through the text with an assignment sheet.

5. If the text does not provide many examples (sample problems, clarifying analogies, example situations, etc.), the instructor can supplement with examples on a margin tab or instruction sheet.

6. If the text does not provide enough illustrations or diagrams, or if the illustrations and diagrams are unclear, the instructor should make new illustrations on an information sheet. Clear illustrations are especially helpful to LEP students.

7. If the learning activities provided are not job-oriented, the instructor should add new activities to the text or on instruction sheets.

8. If there are no activities which students can carry out independently or undertake with other students (without depending on the instructor), the instructor should provide some. LEP students definitely need to have opportunities to collaborate on projects with English-speaking students—a collaboration which is, of course, beneficial to the English-speaking students as well.

Modifications in Physical Appearance

1. If the words in a text are difficult to see, students will probably make little effort to read them. In this case, the instructor can do little more than provide easy-to-read instruction sheets to supplement the text and to help guide the students through it.

2. If key points, important terms, or headings are not easily seen, they should be underlined or marked with a light-colored, felt-tip marker. Again, an assignment sheet can be developed to help guide students through the text.

SAMPLE MODIFIED PAGE
USING STUDENTS' NATIVE LANGUAGE

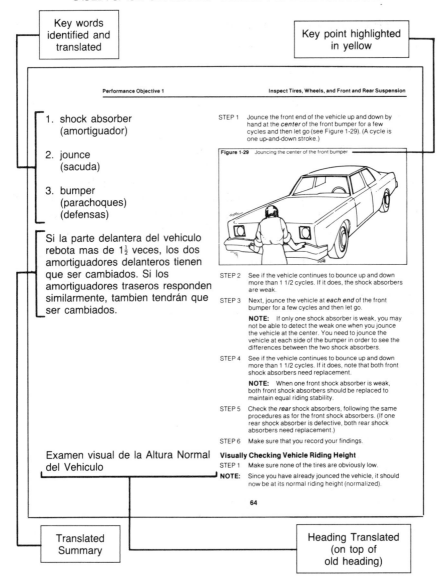

Key words identified and translated

Key point highlighted in yellow

Performance Objective 1   Inspect Tires, Wheels, and Front and Rear Suspension

1. shock absorber
   (amortiguador)

STEP 1   Jounce the front end of the vehicle up and down by hand at the *center* of the front bumper for a few cycles and then let go (see Figure 1-29). (A cycle is one up-and-down stroke.)

2. jounce
   (sacuda)

Figure 1-29   Jouncing the center of the front bumper

3. bumper
   (parachoques)
   (defensas)

Si la parte delantera del vehiculo rebota mas de 1½ veces, los dos amortiguadores delanteros tienen que ser cambiados. Si los amortiguadores traseros responden similarmente, tambien tendrán que ser cambiados.

STEP 2   See if the vehicle continues to bounce up and down more than 1 1/2 cycles. If it does, the shock absorbers are weak.

STEP 3   Next, jounce the vehicle at *each end* of the front bumper for a few cycles and then let go.

NOTE: If only one shock absorber is weak, you may not be able to detect the weak one when you jounce the vehicle at the center. You need to jounce the vehicle at each side of the bumper in order to see the differences between the two shock absorbers.

STEP 4   See if the vehicle continues to bounce up and down more than 1 1/2 cycles. If it does, note that both front shock absorbers need replacement.

NOTE: When one front shock absorber is weak, both front shock absorbers should be replaced to maintain equal riding stability.

STEP 5   Check the *rear* shock absorbers, following the same procedures as for the front shock absorbers. (If one rear shock absorber is defective, both rear shock absorbers need replacement.)

STEP 6   Make sure that you record your findings.

Examen visual de la Altura Normal del Vehiculo

Visually Checking Vehicle Riding Height

STEP 1   Make sure none of the tires are obviously low.

NOTE: Since you have already jounced the vehicle, it should now be at its normal riding height (normalized).

64

Translated Summary

Heading Translated (on top of old heading)

From *Automotive Curriculum, Steering, Suspension, and Wheel Service, Unit 1: Inspection of Steering, Suspension, and Wheel Parts: Student Guide.* Copyright 1979 State of Florida, Department of State. Used with permission of Florida State University, the Center for Studies in Vocational Education.

SAMPLE MODIFIED PAGE
USING SIMPLIFIED ENGLISH

** Excerpt from a vocational text:

To produce a single flare of the correct size:

* Insert tubing into the flaring tool so it extends above the surface of the tool 1/3 of that distance, which is equal to the depth of the flare, Figure 3-5. Tighten the spinner down on the tubing end so that the tubing is gradually worked into a flare, using a back and forth motion. First, put a drop or two of REFRIGERANT OIL on the spinner where it contacts the tubing; then tighten the spinner 1/2 or 3/4 of a turn and back it approximately 1/4 of a turn. Advance it another 3/4 of a turn. In this way, a tubing flare of accurate contour is made with no danger of the tubing cracking.

* Be sure to put the nut on the tube before the flare is made because it cannot be installed on the tubing after the tube has been flared.

Modification:

Flaring

1. Put the nut on the tubing. Make sure the threads of the nut face the short end of the tubing.
2. Put the tubing into the flaring tool. Make sure the tubing extends above the tool.
3. Tighten the spinner down to the end of the tubing.
4. Tighten the spinner 1/2 to 3/4 of a turn.
5. Untighten the spinner 1/4 turn.
6. Tighten the spinner another 3/4 turn.

** From *The Vocational ESL Handbook*, by Joan E. Friedenberg and Curtis H. Bradley, 1984, Newbury House Publishers, Inc., Rowley, MA 01969. Reprinted by permission by the publisher.

CHECKLIST FOR EVALUATING
ENGLISH VOCATIONAL MATERIALS
FOR BILINGUAL VOCATIONAL INSTRUCTION

Name of Text: _____

Author: _____

Publisher: _____

Last Copyright: _____

Name of Course: _____

School: _____

Brief Description of Students:

	Yes	No ▶	If no, on what pages?
(Language of Text)			
1. Avoids overly-complex terminology	☐	☐	☐
2. Terms complex enough for job	☐	☐	☐
3. Explains terms adequately	☐	☐	☐
4. Avoids slang and uncommon words	☐	☐	☐
5. Uses simple sentences	☐	☐	☐

Suggested Modifications in Language:

(Bias)   Yes No ▶ Pages

6. Illustrations have multi-ethnic representation ☐ ☐ ☐

7. Females and males illustrated equally ☐ ☐ ☐

8. Language free of culture and sex stereotyping ☐ ☐ ☐

9. Learning activities for all cultures ☐ ☐ ☐

Suggested Modifications to Eliminate Bias:

(Content)   Yes No ▶ Pages

10. Consistent with course objectives ☐ ☐ ☐

11. Accurate and up-to-date ☐ ☐ ☐

12. Follows logical sequence ☐ ☐ ☐

13. Free of unnecessary detail ☐ ☐ ☐

14. Plenty of examples ☐ ☐ ☐

15. Plenty of clear illustrations ☐ ☐ ☐

16. Job-oriented activities ☐ ☐ ☐

17. Activities for independent practice ☐ ☐ ☐

18. Activities for cooperative practice ☐ ☐ ☐

Suggested Modifications in Content:

(Physical Appearance)   Yes   No ▶   Pages

19. Words easy to see   ☐   ☐   ☐

20. Headings, key points, and terms easy
    to spot   ☐   ☐   ☐

Suggested Modifications in Physical Appearance:

PRACTICE

Evaluate and describe how you might modify an English vocational text, manufacturer's handbook, or similar vocational instructional materials using the evaluation checklist provided in this chapter.

CHAPTER **4**

Evaluating Bilingual
and Non-English Vocational Materials
for Bilingual Vocational Instruction

WHAT ARE BILINGUAL
AND NON-ENGLISH VOCATIONAL MATERIALS?

There are generally three kinds of bilingual and non-English vocational instructional materials:

- Books containing complete texts in two languages, usually with the English text on one side of the page and the translated version on the other side.
- English vocational texts which have separate translated versions.
- Imported non-English vocational texts which have no English counterparts.

Advantages of Using Bilingual
and Non-English Vocational Materials

1. They can serve as good references for vocational instructors (or employers) who wish to learn some of the technical terminology in the other language(s).
2. They can be good resources for limited-English proficient students as they can be used to supplement English materials and to clarify various points.
3. They can assist vocational counselors, instructors, and placement specialists in assessing an LEP student's level of technical knowledge.

4. They can help bilingual and LEP students prepare for exams.
5. They can allow non-English-proficient students to immediately begin vocational instruction while they are in the process of learning English.
6. They can contribute to the self-concepts of language minority students by showing them that their native language is academically worthwhile.

Disadvantages of Using Bilingual and Non-English Vocational Materials

1. Imported materials sometimes are not technologically suitable for a U.S. vocational setting.
2. Imported materials are sometimes difficult to find, expensive, and long in arriving.
3. Imported materials often have no English counterparts and are rarely cross-referenced.
4. Many LEP students are unfamiliar with the technical terminology in their native language.
5. Many LEP students cannot read in their native language.
6. Many technical terms differ across dialects, and speakers of one dialect may be unfamiliar with terms in another.
7. It is not advisable for LEP students to rely *solely* on their native language when trying to acquire job skills in the U.S.

EVALUATING MATERIALS

When evaluating bilingual and non-English vocational materials for possible adoption for bilingual vocational instruction, the instructor should refer to the same questions of language, bias, content, and physical appearance that were posed for evaluating English vocational materials (see Chapter 3). In addition to these, however, there are other determinations which must be made in regard to these materials, particularly in the areas of language and content.

Language

1. Is the non-English text grammatically correct (e.g., spelling, structure, meaning, etc.)?
2. Are dialect variations in terminology included?

Content

1. Is the measuring system appropriate for a U.S. job setting?
2. If imported, are the materials appropriate for a U.S. technical setting?
3. If imported, can the text be cross-referenced with an American text?

CHECKLIST FOR EVALUATING BILINGUAL AND NON-ENGLISH VOCATIONAL MATERIALS FOR BILINGUAL VOCATIONAL INSTRUCTION

Name of Text: _____

Author: _____

Publisher: _____

Last Copyright: _____

Name of Course: _____

School: _____

Brief Description of Students (reminder: ability to read in the first language is an important consideration):

		If no, on
(Language(s) of Text)	Yes No ▶	what pages?
	(English)	

(Language(s) of Text)

Applicable only to bilingual materials or materials with English counterparts.

1. English text avoids overly complex terminology ☐ ☐ ▭

2. English terms complex enough for job ☐ ☐ ▭

3. English text explains terms adequately ☐ ☐ ▭

4. English text avoids slang/uses simple sentences ☐ ☐ ▭

5. English text uses simple sentences ☐ ☐ ▭

6. Non-English text is grammatically correct (i.e. spelling, structure, meaning, etc.) ☐ ☐ ▭

7. Dialect variations in the native language included ☐ ☐ ▭

(Bias)

8. Illustrations have multi-ethnic representation ☐ ☐ ▭

9. Females and males illustrated equally ☐ ☐ ▭

10. Languages free of culture and sex stereotyping ☐ ☐ ▭

11. Learning activities for all cultures ☐ ☐ ▭

(Content)

12. Consistent with course objectives ☐ ☐ ▭

13. Accurate and up-to-date ☐ ☐ ▭

	Yes	No ▶	If no, on what pages?
(Content)		(English)	
14. Follows logical sequence	☐	☐	☐
15. Free of unnecessary detail	☐	☐	☐
16. Plenty of examples	☐	☐	☐
17. Plenty of clear illustrations	☐	☐	☐
18. Job-oriented activities	☐	☐	☐
19. Activities for independent practice	☐	☐	☐
20. Activities for cooperative practice	☐	☐	☐
21. Measuring system appropriate	☐	☐	☐
22. Technologically appropriate for U.S.	☐	☐	☐
23. Cross-referenced with English text	☐	☐	☐
(Physical Appearance)			
24. Words easy to see	☐	☐	☐
25. Headings, key points, and terms easy to spot	☐	☐	☐

FINAL ASSESSMENT

Text:

	Yes	No
Should be adopted for regular student use	☐	☐
Should be available for students' reference only	☐	☐
Would be helpful to instructor for reference	☐	☐

Should not be adopted ☐   Reasons:

A SELECTED LIST OF PUBLISHERS
AND DISTRIBUTORS OF BILINGUAL
AND NON-ENGLISH VOCATIONAL MATERIALS

Publisher	*Vocational Areas*	*Language(s)*
BILINGUAL PUBLICATIONS CO. 1966 Broadway New York, NY 10023	Air conditioning and refrigeration, auto mechanics, business education, commercial correspondence, electronics, health occupations, home economics, TV & radio repair.	Spanish
BROLET PRESS 18 John Street New York, NY 10038	Electronics	Creole Portuguese Spanish
CHILTON BOOK CO. Radnor, PA 19089	Auto mechanics	Spanish
EUROPEAN BOOK CO. 925 Larkin Street San Francisco, CA 94109	Agribusiness, air conditioning & refrigeration, auto mechanics, construction, data processing, electronics, health occupations, sewing, TV & radio repair, voc. teacher education	Spanish
HEFFERNAN'S SUPPLY CO. 926 Fredericksburg Road Box 5309 San Antonio, TX 78201	Accounting, agribusiness, auto mechanics, commercial correspondence, construction, data processing, drafting, electronics, TV & radio repair.	Spanish
LAB VOLT SYSTEMS P.O. Box 686 Farmingdale, NJ 07727	Electricity & electronics	Multilingual

Publisher	Vocational Areas	Language(s)
McGRAW-HILL 1221 Avenue of the Americas New York, NY 10022	Business education, drafting, machine shop, welding	Spanish
MILADY PUBLISHING CORP. 3839 White Plains Road Bronx, NY 10467	Cosmetology	Spanish
MINERVA BOOK COMPANY 137 West 14 Street New York, NY 10011	Air conditioning & refrigeration, auto mechanics, business education, health occupations, TV & radio repair	Spanish
QUALITY BOOK CO. 400 Anthony Trail Northbrook, IL 60062	Auto mechanics, construction, electronics, TV & radio repair	Spanish
RICHARDS ROSEN PRESS 29 East 21st Street New York, NY 10010	Employability skills	Spanish
SOUTH-WESTERN PUBLISHING CO. Dpto. de Ediciones en Español 5101 Madison Road Cincinnati, OH 45227	Business education, health occupations, industrial arts	Spanish
THE FRENCH & SPANISH BOOK CORPORATION 610 Fifth Avenue New York, NY 10020	Agriculture, auto repair, business education, carpentry, construction, cosmetology, data processing, electricity, electronics, graphic arts, health occupations, heating, home economics, hotel & restaurant, photography, printing, real estate, radio & TV repair, refrigeration	French Spanish

PRACTICE

1. Evaluate a bilingual or non-English vocational text, manufacturer's handbook, or similar instructional material using the evaluation checklist provided in this chapter.

2. Provide a justification for your final assessment.

CHAPTER **5**

Developing Instruction Sheets
for Bilingual Vocational Education

Instruction sheets are written teaching aids designed to be used by individual students. They are especially useful in multicultural vocational education settings where the students' abilities vary with regard to both occupational experience and proficiency in English. We will begin with a discussion of the advantages and characteristics of instruction sheets, followed by descriptions and examples of how they can be used and developed in multilingual settings.

ADVANTAGES OF INSTRUCTION SHEETS

An oral presentation is easily prepared by the instructor, and within two-way communication, can be the easiest method of communicating, particularly because it can be made highly sensitive to each individual student's needs. It does have disadvantages, however, as it requires the constant presence and attention of the instructor. Additionally, lacking permanence, it requires large amounts of repetition on the part of the instructor. All of this naturally tends to make the learner too dependent on the instructor.

Writing as a means of communication is permanent and can easily be duplicated and/or modified as required. Its permanence permits the student to follow the directions for the learning activity in the absence of the instructor and to review them as often as necessary. The ability to duplicate the material allows the instruction to cover an indefinitely large group. A highly important additional advantage of written direction of learning is that it trains students in a means of learning that is readily available to them after leaving the classroom environment.

Textbooks often require too much reading in order to obtain a few essential facts. In addition, the text might be too technical for the reading ability of the student. Instruction sheets are designed to provide precisely the amount of information that a student needs at a particular time, and to provide that information in a manner appropriate to the reading level of the student. For LEP students, this means that all or part of a particular instruction sheet might be in their native language(s).

Through selective combination of oral and written direction of learning, the advantages of both can be secured and the disadvantages of each minimized. Learning through writing is most effective when it is organized in the form of instruction sheets, rather than in book form. Instruction sheets present the student successively with a limited object of attention, and they can be arranged and rearranged in any sequence that seems desirable for the individual student.

CHARACTERISTICS OF EFFECTIVE INSTRUCTION SHEETS

Instruction sheets must be written in clear, simple, and concise language. They should be profusely illustrated because diagrams and sketches are often more readily comprehended by both LEP and English-speaking students. They should also be formatted to avoid large masses of words so as not to present the student with an overwhelming amount of material to learn all at once.

TYPES OF INSTRUCTION SHEETS

A wide variety of instruction sheets is used throughout vocational-technical education. The following will provide a brief description of some of the most frequently used ones.

Information Sheets

Information sheets provide scientific and other pertinent information which students need to understand the processes and procedures they must deal with. Information sheets may take the form of technical information closely related to an operation, basic scientific principles, production processes, reference tables, or other information relevant to the training program. The information sheet is most often concerned with the "why" of a procedure, as contrasted with the "what" of a job sheet and the "how" of an operation sheet.

Operation Sheets

Operation sheets each contain the directions and information needed for performing one operation. These directions should be given step by step in the order in which they are to be performed. There should be one paragraph to each step, each paragraph numbered serially in order and separated by double spaces. Numbers should be used on instruction sheets only for numbering the steps in a procedure.

Sketches and diagrams should be included whenever they will aid in understanding. Often most of the story can be told with sketches and diagrams. Sketches should usually be small and clear and should be placed to the right of the steps they illustrate.

All information and precautions needed in the effective performance of the operation should be given at the point in the procedure where it will be needed. No other information should be included.

The language should be simple, clear, and direct; no unnecessary words should be used. All verbs should be in the command form, e.g.:

> "Select a . . . ."
> "Cut a . . . ."
> "Drill the . . . ."

Job Sheets

Job sheets provide all of the information required to complete a particular job. Job sheets are *not* intended to explain *how* to perform the operations involved in the job; they only *list* the operations. Where necessary, reference is made to appropriate operation sheets where detailed information on how to perform operations is provided. In addition to listing every operation, a job sheet will provide the necessary drawings, specifications, tools, material, and equipment, CHECK POINT (where the student must check with the instructor before continuing the job), and safety precautions.

Job sheets should be written like operation sheets. The directions given above for operation sheets regarding numbering and spacing of paragraphing and using simple, clear, direct language also apply to job sheets.

Cross-references should be inserted where appropriate to interconnect the operation sheets, e.g.:

"See operation sheet #____"

Job Plan Sheets

Job plan sheets are essentially job sheets for advanced students. In the initial stages of learning, the instructor provides the student with a job sheet that lists every step on the job, as well as the tools, material, and equipment necessary to perform the job. As the student progresses, part of vocational education involves having the student determine this information prior to beginning the job. Thus, job plan sheets are forms that students complete to verify that they understand every operation in a particular job, as well as the tools, materials, and equipment necessary to complete it.

Assignment Sheets

Assignment sheets are used to direct students' study. These study activities may include reading selected passages and answering questions designed to bring out the significant points to be learned. They may include work in the library, in other shops, or outside of school. Directions for such activities should be given on assignment sheets.

Because of their diversified nature, no specific directions can be given for writing assignment sheets. However, some general guidelines can be provided. They should give clear, concise directions for carrying out the activity step by step. All unnecessary words should be eliminated from the directions. The format should be kept open and free from solid masses of reading matter. Paragraphs should be short and separated from each other by double spaces. Sketches and diagrams should be used whenever they will serve better than words.

Problem Sheets

Problem sheets are appropriately used to give learners practice in the exercise of judgment in the solution of types of problems found in the field of instruction.

By problems we do not merely mean situations which involve numerical calculation, but any situation which involves the exercise of judgment, reflective thought, or reasoning. The goal is to foster the development of the students' powers of judgment—an area which most courses of instruction do not give sufficient attention to.

Experiment Sheets

Experiments, as distinct from jobs, are activities designed to bring to the learner an understanding of some phenomenon. Experiments are educationally appropriate when the learner needs a clearer or more vivid understanding of that phenomenon. Experiments are often used, indeed often over-used, in science instruction, and they should be much more freely used in most vocational instruction.

Used appropriately, experiments are a very effective method to foster the learning process. A few examples should serve to illustrate this point. An appreciation of the reason for boring pilot holes for wood screws can be made highly vivid by an experiment involving screws in scraps of wood with and without pilot holes. Similarly, an appreciation of how an electric fuse works can be more effectively developed by an experiment in blowing fuses (in a circuit suitably protected against damage) than by a mere description of the purpose of fuses.

Experiment sheets should outline clearly and concisely, in numbered steps, exactly what learners are expected to do. Students should not be told what they are to find, as this robs the experiment of interest. The points which students are to observe should be outlined by questions which they must answer. Experiment sheets are similar to operation sheets in format and wording.

DESCRIPTIONS AND SAMPLES
OF INSTRUCTION SHEETS

Following are descriptions and samples of each of the most frequently used types of instruction sheets. Sample forms included in this chapter are meant to provide the reader with a suggested guide to the development of each of these kinds of instruction sheets. However, they are not meant to be limiting in any way, and instructors are encouraged to adapt them to their own specific needs and preferences.

The Information Sheet: Description

Skilled workers must know the "why" as well as the "how" of their occupation. Just as operation sheets are used to describe the "how," information sheets are prepared to explain the "why." If each operation lesson is material for an operation sheet, each information lesson is material for a possible information sheet. Each information unit in an occupation is a potential information sheet. Some representative information units from various occupations are:

Occupation	*Information*
Baker	The action of yeast on bread dough.
Cosmetologist	The purpose and use of astringents.
Dressmaker	Linen: what it is and where to use it.
Electrician	The principle of the transformer.
Mechanic	The principle of the differential in an automobile.
Plumber	Cast iron pipe types, sizes, and uses.
Printer	The point system of measurement.

Information sheets are to be studied, not followed, and their content should be fairly informal. They should be both easy and interesting to read. Ideally, they should tell a story, have a theme, and reveal continuity and sequence in the material presented.

An instructor should prepare and use an information sheet if any of the following conditions exist:

- The necessity to duplicate information only available in a single copy.
- The necessity to present up-to-date information not included in the basic references used in the course.
- The necessity to supplement information in basic references which do not completely cover the subject.
- The necessity to condense material which is too lengthy.
- The necessity to consolidate materials gathered from several sources.
- The necessity to translate "why" information into the native language(s) of LEP students.
- The necessity to translate terminology into the native language(s) of LEP students.
- The necessity to simplify language used in the basic references.

Information Sheet: Format

SCHOOL _____   Information Sheet No. _____

COURSE _____   (Use same no. as in course of study.)

_____

Title of information to be presented should be inserted here.
_____

INFORMATION: 1. Should be written to suit level of student.

                       2. Sentences and paragraphs should be concise.

                       3. Illustrations should be used where they will assist in clarifying the information.

                       4. Material should be organized and presented in a logical sequence.

                       5. Material should be of sufficient length and complexity to challenge the student.

Information Sheet: Sample

Ellen Hansford Adult Center   Information Sheet #22

Course: Small Engine Repair

The Fuel Mixture

The fuel we use is gasoline.

Gasoline comes from the pump as a liquid. However, for the engine to work, the gasoline must be vaporized or made like air. Gasoline becomes vaporized when it is mixed with air. The amount of air and gasoline that is mixed is called the *fuel-air ratio*.[1] A mixture of 15 pounds of air to 1 pound of gasoline is considered an *average mixture*.[2] A mixture that contains less air is called a *rich mixture*,[3] say 10 to 1. A mixture that contains more air is called a *lean mixture*,[4] say 18 to 1.

---

(1) *Razón de combustible y aire:*
La cantidad de aire y gasolina que se mezcla.
(2) *Mezcla Promedio:*
Mezcla de quince libras de air por cada libra de gasolina.
(3) *Mezcla Rica:*
Una mezcla con menos aire que la cantidad promedio.
(4) *Mezcla Pobre:*
Una mezcla con mas aire que la cantidad promedio.

> The instructor of this class of Spanish and English-speaking students provided a translation of the contents of this information sheet in Spanish to benefit those who are LEP.

Information Sheet: Sample

Roberto Clemente Center   Information Sheet #2

COURSE: *Cabinetmaking*

Selecting a Screwdriver

The cabinetmaker must select the exact screwdriver for each task. The screwdriver blade must match the head of the screw. If the blade is not the correct size, damage might be done to the head of the screw or to the mounting surface.

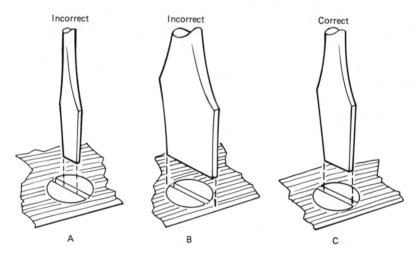

Incorrect   Incorrect   Correct

A   B   C

The Operation Sheet: Description

An operation is one step in the process of performing a job. Giving a manicure is a job, but greeting the patron who is getting the manicure is an operation. Operation units in a trade may be, and usually are, lesson topics, or demonstrations to be presented by the teacher. As mentioned previously, the teacher may give the lesson in two ways—by demonstrating how to greet a patron, or by giving the students a written or printed sheet explaining how to greet a patron, i.e. the corresponding operation sheet. Accordingly, any operation in a trade may be put in the form of a written instruction. Some representative operations from various trades are:

Occupation	*Information*
Auto Mechanic	How to gap a spark plug.
Baker	How to cream sugar, shortening, and salt.
Cosmetologist	How to greet a patron.
Electrician	How to make a saddle bend in 1/2" conduit.
Machinist	How to sharpen a drill.
Plumber	How to cut pipe with a pipe cutter.
Printer	How to ink a press.
Sheetmetal Worker	How to wire an edge.

An operation sheet tells how to do something, just as the instructions and directions that accompany a toy or a game tell the purchaser how to use the toy or play the game. A good operation sheet must:

- be written in simple, clear, and concise language,
- be well-illustrated and picture each step or point that may cause difficulty,
- be arranged in a logical learning order like the lesson itself,
- contain safety precautions at pertinent points, and
- explain and illustrate or translate all new terms and names.

Operation sheets give a detailed account of the procedure involved in carrying out specific trade tasks. To be effective, they must be so clear and explicit in the directions they give that, with the use of the sheet alone, a good student with the prerequisite experience could carry on the new performance with reasonable success.

The operation sheet is designed to supplement the teacher's demonstration and instruction. As such, it serves varying functions for different students. It helps the average pupil to individually practice what he or she has learned after a demonstration has been given. It may serve as initial instruction for advanced students who are capable of moving ahead of the others in the group. It helps the slower student by providing a means of reviewing the instructions previously given by the teacher.

Preparation of Operation Sheets

1. Title: A *brief* but specific term which identifies the operation as distinct from every other operation. For convenience, place this in the upper right hand corner of the sheet, together with a series index number for ready reference and filing.

2. Statement of Purpose of Operation: A brief description of what learners are to be able to do and what they should know when they have mastered this unit.

3. List of Tools and Materials: Include type and other descriptive information about tools and materials. Where one size of an item is regularly used, sizes should also be given. Since operation sheets apply to a wide variety of jobs, care should be taken not to restrict the use of the sheet by the list of tools provided.

4. Steps of Operation: List the steps to be followed in the best (most logical) order possible. Describe in simple, direct language exactly what is to be done. There should be enough instructions so that the majority of learners who are going to use the sheet can do so without further explanation from the instructor. Use illustrations where they will make the instructions clearer; place them to the right of the step they apply to. Provide information necessary to the performance of the operation on the sheet at the point where it will be needed. Number the steps and use spacing to separate them into distinct items. Avoid including separable steps in one item. Avoid using unnecessary words. Make statements clear and concise. Define and translate new terms and use the language of the learners. This may require the development of

more than one form of the sheet for different learners. All or part of an operation sheet may be in the students' native language(s), depending upon the needs of the students and the goals of the instructional program. Keep in mind that LEP students who are not familiar with some terms in English may not be familiar with the same terms in their native language, either. In this case, translation is not always helpful, but careful definition and illustration (in English) are. It is more useful to use a translation when the students have had some occupational experience in their native language(s) and are already familiar with the terms in that language. In the case of a mixed class, a single bilingual or multilingual operation sheet could meet the needs of most, if not all, students.

Operation Sheet: Format

SCHOOL _____   Operation No. _____
COURSE _____   (Use same no. as in course of
                                study.)

Insert name of operation

SKETCH/DRAWING AND/OR   Provide, if necessary.
INTRODUCTORY INFORMATION:

MATERIALS: List materials needed
                               to perform operation.

TOOLS AND EQUIPMENT: List tools and
                               equipment needed.

PROCEDURE: State each step in the
                               operation.

                               Steps should be stated
                               clearly and concisely
                               in occupational terms.

                               List steps in proper
                               sequence.

                               Number steps
                               consecutively.

                               Safety and key points
                               should be listed with
                               steps where they
                               apply.

                               Double space between
                               each step.

CHECK POINT:

A CHECK POINT may occur at any step in the procedure where the instructor desires to check students before allowing them to proceed.

There may be more than one CHECK POINT in the operation.

Place the words CHECK POINT in the left margin at the point in the procedure where the student is to be checked by the instructor before proceeding with the next step.

Operation Sheet: Sample

SCHOOL <u>Fannie Gelman Sr. High</u>   Operation Sheet <u>22</u>

COURSE <u>Beginning Machine Shop</u>

How to chip metal

INTRODUCTION:

Chipping is the process of removing metal by means of a cold chisel and hammer. The use of the shaper, milling machine, and planer are more efficient methods of removing metal accurately and rapidly, but the use of the chisel is necessary on many jobs where accuracy is not important and only a small amount of metal is to be removed.

TOOLS AND EQUIPMENT:

Cold chisel   Machinist's hammer
Machinist's vise   Goggles

SAFETY PRECAUTIONS:

1. Goggles should be worn during the chipping process.
2. Make sure that the chisel head is not "mushroomed," as particles may break off and cause a personal injury.

PROCEDURE:

1. Mount the work firmly in the vise; use soft copper jaw if the work has finished surface.
2. Hold the chisel with the thumb and fingers of one hand so that the head end extends above the hand.
3. Place the cutting edge of the chisel on the surface of the job where the cut is to be made. The chisel should be held at a cutting angle of approximately 45 degrees.
4. Grasp the hammer, with the other hand, near the end of the handle so that it can be swung with an easy forearm movement.
5. Strike the head of the chisel with a firm sharp blow.
6. Reset the cutting edge of the chisel on the work and repeat the above steps.

Como cincelar metal

INTRODUCCION:

Cincelar es el proceso de remover metal por medio de un cincel y un martillo de ajustador. El uso de la limadora, la fresadora, y la cepilladora son métodos mas eficientes para remover metal mas preciso y rapidamente, pero el uso del cincel es necesario en muchos trabajos en los cuales la precisión no es muy importante y cuando no hay que remover mucho metal.

HERRAMIENTAS Y EQUIPO:

Cincel	Martillo de ajustador
Prensa	Anteojos de protección

PRECAUCIONES DE SEGURIDAD:

1. Los anteojos de protección deben ser usados durante todo el proceso.
2. Asegúrese de que el cincel (chisel) no se haya "floreado" puesto que algunas partículas pueden desprenderse y causar heridas al (a la) operador(a).

PROCEDIMIENTO:

1. Coloque la pieza en la prensa (vise); use soportes de cobre si la pieza tiene acabado liso.
2. Sostenga el cincel (chisel) con el pulgar y los dedos de la mano izquierda, de tal forma que la cabeza del cincel esté por encima de la mano.
3. Coloque la punta aguda del cincel (chisel) sobre la superficie de la pieza donde el corte se va a hacer. El cincel debe sostenerse a un ángulo aproximado de 45° con respecto a la superficie de la pieza.
4. Sostenga el martillo (hammer) cerca de la punta del mango (handle) de tal forma que la acción de martillar sea efectuada con un movimiento fácil del brazo.
5. Golpée la cabeza del cincel (chisel) con un golpe firme del martillo (hammer).
6. Colque la punta aguda del cincel (chisel) nuevamente sobre la pieza y repita los pasos anteriores.

This was developed for a class with both Spanish-speaking and English-speaking vocational students. Since some of the Spanish-speaking students had previous occupational experience in Machine Shop, the instructor found it useful to include a Spanish translation of the names of the tools and equipment. The instructor also provided a translation of the procedure, which was beneficial to all the Spanish-speaking students. Notice that *English* translations of the tools were provided in the Spanish part for the benefit of the Spanish-speaking students who were unfamiliar with the names of the tools in Spanish.

The Job Sheet: Description

In vocational education, learners are usually assigned actual jobs to perform under varying degrees of supervision. To help ensure success and high standards, the instructor prepares a job sheet for each such job. Job sheets are particularly useful in classes where different levels of instruction occur at the same time.

Occupation	*Job*
Auto mechanic	Reline and adjust the brakes on a car.
Baker	Make an order of cupcakes.
Cosmetologist	Give a manicure.
Electrician	Install an extra convenience outlet.
Machinist	Make a flanged bushing.
Plumber	Run in a roof vent.
Sheet Metal Worker	Make a section of sheet metal cornices.

As used in the occupation itself, a job sheet may be quite simple, containing a blueprint to sketch and providing only the minimum information needed for the job. In a sense, the tickets, shop blueprint, work orders, and similar items used in an occupation are job sheets. However, the learner in early training needs more information than the experienced worker. For that reason the job sheets used in training are designed to help the trainee learn *how* to do the job, as well as to serve as a job assignment. Job sheets used for instructional purposes usually contain:

- a statement of the job to be done;
- a list of materials and equipment needed;
- a procedure outline;
- directions for checking the finished work;
- pictures, diagrams, working drawings, and sketches to show what is wanted; and
- pictures, diagrams, and sketches to clarify any anticipated difficulties the learner may have.

Gradually, the job sheets given a learner should become more like the job ticket, work order, or blueprints that will be used in the occupation.

Some job form or job sheet should be prepared for each job that will be taught in a course. If the instructor finds it necessary to provide the students with job sheets in their native language, the English version should always be included, too. Also, since it is unlikely that the students will have bilingual forms and work orders when they become workers, the instructor must attempt to "wean" them from using their native language as soon as possible.

Job Sheet: Format

SCHOOL _____   Job No. _____
COURSE _____   (Use same no. as in course of
                               study.)

Insert name of job

SKETCH OR DRAWING: Provide drawing or make
                          sketch, if necessary.

MATERIALS: List materials needed to
                          perform job.

TOOLS AND EQUIPMENT: List tools and equipment
                          needed to perform job.

PROCEDURE: State each operation or step
                          in the job. Operations should
                          be stated clearly and
                          concisely.

                          List operations in proper
                          sequence.

                          Number operations
                          consecutively.

                          List safety and key points
                          with the operations where
                          they apply.

                          Double space between each
                          operation.

CHECK POINT

A CHECK POINT may occur at any operation in the procedure where the instructor desires to check the trainees before allowing them to proceed.

There may be more than one CHECK POINT in the job.

Place the words CHECK POINT in the left margin at the point in the procedure where the trainee is to be checked by the instructor before proceeding with the next operation.

Job Sheet: Sample

SCHOOL Herbert Tech.   Job Sheet No. 21

COURSE Electric
        Construction

Install Four Receptacles on Same Circuit Using Conduit

MATERIAL: (MATERIALES)	(20) Plastic Anchors (4) Utility Boxes (4) Duplex Receptacles (4) Utility Box Covers (2) 1/2″ Red 90°'s (3) 1/2″ Set Screw T's W/C	(5) 1/2″ EMT Connec- tors (12) 1/2″ EMT Straps 50′ 1/2″ EMT Conduit 100′ #12 TW Black 100′ # 2 TW White 4 Ground Screws

TOOLS AND EQUIPMENT: (HERRAMIENTAS Y EQUIPO)	1/4″ Electric Drill 1/4″ Masonry Bit 6″ Screwdriver Fish Tape	25′ Extension Cord 1/2″ Hickey 7″ Side Cutters

PROCEDURE:
(PROCEDIMIENTO)

1. Determine the location (Determine la localización) (Operation Sheet 5).
2. Mount the boxes (Monte las cajas) (Operation Sheet 4).
3. Install the conduits (Instale los conductos) (Operation Sheet 6).
4. Push the fish tape in conduit (Meta la cinta pescadora en el conducto.)
5. Attach wires to the fish tape (Amarre los alambres a la cinta pescadora).

6. Pull the wire in conduit (Tire los alambres de dentro del conducto).
7. Make all connections (Haga las conecciones) (Operation Sheet 3).
8. Install the outlets (Instale los tomacorrientes).
9. Check the circuit Chequée el circuito) (Operation Sheet 8).
10. Return tools and equipment (Devuela las herramientas y equipo).

The Spanish-speaking students in this class have not had much previous occupational experience in their native language. Therefore, the instructor did not find it useful to provide translations for the names of the materials, tools, and equipment. The students will learn these terms, which are all new to them, in English only. The "procedures" section was provided in Spanish because the students are limited-English-proficient and might not understand the simple verbs (e.g., push, attach, pull, etc.) in English, while they would understand them in Spanish.

The Job Plan Sheet: Description

As students gain knowledge and skill in a trade, the amount and kind of planning expected from them changes. The job plan sheet is intended to take the place of the job sheet as soon as the students have acquired sufficient ability to begin to plan their own work. The job plan sheet the student prepares should be detailed as long as the instructor considers that such detail is essential in the planning needs of the individual student. When the student has progressed to the point where the instructor feels confident in reducing the amount of detailed planning for an individual, the instructor can change the structure of the planning, varying kind and amount to fit the need of the individual student. Eventually the job plan sheet will have the same format as a typical work order used in a specific trade.

The job plan sheet is a student aid consisting of a skeleton blank sheet on which the student, for the job at hand:

- prepares a bill of material listing the amount, kind, and size of material required;
- lists operations in their proper sequence;
- lists tools and equipment needed;
- estimates the time required to do the job;
- performs the necessary mathematical computations;
- prepares freehand sketches as required; and
- lists for study the assignment sheets pertinent to the job.

Job Plan Sheet: Format

STUDENT'S NAME _____

JOB PLAN SHEET

SCHOOL _____   Job Plan No. _____
COURSE _____   (Use same no. as on progress
chart.)

Insert name of job

SKETCH OR DRAWING: If instructor deems necessary, student makes sketch or drawing as directed.

MATERIALS: List materials needed to perform job.

TOOLS AND EQUIPMENT: List tools and equipment needed to perform job.

PROCEDURE: State each operation or step in the job. Operations should be stated clearly and concisely.

List operations in proper sequence.

Number operations consecutively.

List safety and key points with operations where they apply.

CHECK POINT:

A CHECK POINT may occur at any operation in the procedure where the instructor desires to check the students before allowing them to proceed.

There may be more than one CHECK POINT in the job.

The instructor should draw a red line in the left margin at the point in the procedure where the student is to be checked by the instructor before proceeding with the next operation.

Estimated time: _____ hours.
  (Determined by student,
  subject to instructor's
  approval)
Actual time: _____ hours.
  (Clock hours to complete
  job)

_____
Approved by Instructor
  (Initialed or signed
  before work is started)

Job Plan Sheet: Sample

STUDENT'S NAME _____

JOB PLAN SHEET

SCHOOL <u>D. Roberts Vo-Tech Institute</u>   Job Plan No. _____
COURSE <u>Air Conditioning and Refrigeration</u>

SKETCH OR DRAWING:
(ESQUEMA O DIBUJO)

MATERIALS:
(MATERIALES)

TOOLS AND EQUIPMENT:
(HERRAMIENTAS Y EQUIPO)

PROCEDURE:
(PROCEDIMIENTO)

CHECK POINT:
(PUNTO DE CHEQUEO)

Estimated time: _____ hours.
Tiempo estimado: _____

Actual time: _____ hours.   Approved by Instructor
Tiempo gastado: _____   (Firma del Instructor)

> The instructor of this class of English- and Spanish-speaking students will accept the completed Job Plan Sheet in either language. The instructor will be able to obtain an English translation from a colleague, aide, or more advanced bilingual student.

The Assignment Sheet: Description

The shop or laboratory often provides only a limited opportunity for the learner to apply the instruction received from the teacher. Since affording students the opportunity to apply what they have learned is the essence of good teaching, any device which provides application supplemental to the shop or laboratory work itself will be advantageous. Assignment sheets are used for this. For example, after receiving instruction on reading a micrometer, the learner should have an opportunity to actually practice this new skill in order to become proficient at it. However, frequent opportunities to do this in the shop or laboratory immediately after a lesson are unlikely. Hence, a sheet of drawings (i.e. an assignment sheet) showing a variety of micrometer settings could be given to the learner to provide repetitive application of this skill. Other possibilities for assignment sheets in several representative occupations are:

Occupations	*Information*
Auto Mechanic	Take specific gravity and voltage readings of several storage batteries and describe the condition of each from the data obtained.
Commercial Artist:	Collect several samples of printing that illustrate the difference between the optical and the geometrical center of the page.
Dressmaker:	Examine the samples of textiles furnished, and fill out the data requested in the space provided.
Electrician:	Determine which sections of the National Electrical Code apply to a particular installation.
Foundry Worker:	Calculate the estimated weights of the iron castings which are to be made from the accompanying drawings.
Printer:	Determine the cost of the stock for the jobs described.

Assignment sheets can utilize a variety of techniques and types of experiences. For example, they may consist of:

- a series of questions to be answered,
- bills of material to make up,
- an interview to be conducted,
- films or tapes to study,
- drawings to analyze,
- data to study and interpret,
- procedures to plan, and
- an observation or investigation to be done.*

The purpose of assignment sheets is to get students to do things. Hence, all the principles of motivation, the feeling of need for the experience, and an understanding of its purpose and value by the student are essential for effective results. Thus, it is important that assignment sheets conform to the characteristics of effective instruction sheets; namely, that they be written in clear, simple, and concise language and avoid appearing like an overwhelming mass of words. In addition, they must contain a motivating introduction that helps students understand the goals and importance of the activities to be performed.

Assignment sheets help the student to secure additional experiences. They provide the kind of repetitive activities which are essential in the development of judgment and mental skills. In general, assignment sheets are most effective when they closely follow any instruction which calls for students to apply the skill(s) contained in the instruction.

Identifying Characteristics of an Assignment Sheet

1. Frequently *called a study guide.*
2. May have the *appearance of a quiz* or *examination.*
3. Usually *consists* of *questions, problems,* or *related exercises.*
4. *Directs* the *study* of the *student.*
5. Tells the student what to do, but concerning *non-manipulative work only.*
6. Includes a source of information that enables the student to complete the assignment.

---

* Give some help to the learner on how to go about it. For example, a sheet requesting data would have a suggested form for recording the data in an organized way. A sheet on conducting an interview would indicate the best procedure to follow.

Assignment Sheet: Format

SCHOOL _____   Assignment Sheet No. __26__

COURSE _____   (Use same no. as in course of study.)

Insert title of assignment

INTRODUCTORY INFORMATION:	Short, concise statement for the purpose of motivating the student to complete the assignment.
ASSIGNED SOURCE OF INFORMATION:	State the source of information that will enable the student to complete the assignment. This might be reading printed matter, viewing a film, listening to a tape, or observing a live or simulated activity.
QUESTIONS, PROBLEMS, OR ACTIVITY:	The assignment should adequately cover the specific subject in this assignment sheet. Questions and problems should be stated clearly and concisely. Students should clearly understand what they are expected to do.

Assignment Sheet: Sample

SCHOOL Wayne Community   Assignment Sheet No. 18
        College
COURSE Practical Nursing   Instructor: Ms. Santiago

Factors Contributing to the Expansion of the Nursing Role

INTRODUCTION: The role of the nurse is in a state of
                       almost revolutionary change as
                       nurses in both acute and ambulatory
                       patient care settings take on a variety
                       of new responsibilities. These new
                       responsibilities include functions that
                       until recently were considered
                       medical rather than nursing
                       functions. It is important that nurses
                       understand the factors contributing to
                       the expansion of the role of the
                       nurse.

ASSIGNED READING: Read pages 53 to 60 in Bullough, B.,
                       *The Law and the Expanding Nurse
                       Role*. New York: Appleton-Century-
                       Crofts, 1975.

QUESTIONS AND   Write a one-paragraph answer to
ACTIVITIES: each of the following:

                       1. What was the contribution of
                          collegiate nursing education
                          programs to the expansion of the
                          nursing role?

                       2. Explain the contribution of the
                          career ladder concept.

                       3. Name three factors outside of the
                          profession that contributed to the
                          expansion of the nursing role.

Since this textbook is written only in English, the instructor did not find it useful to provide the assignment sheet questions and activities in the students' native language(s). In addition, students can read the text with the use of a bilingual dictionary without the pressure of time. Since there are students who can speak or read English, but who have difficulty writing, this instructor allowed the students to do the activities in their native language.

Assignment Sheet: Sample

Bradberg Tech   Ms. Stressler

COURSE <u>Commercial</u>   Assignment Sheet No. <u> 12 </u>
        <u>Refrigeration</u>

The Maintenance Schedule

INTRODUCTION: We have studied and discussed the
                     suggested maintenance schedule for a
                     commercial refrigeration system. This
                     assignment is designed to help you
                     learn whether the recommended
                     practices that we have studied are
                     actually followed in the industry.

ASSIGNED SOURCE   After obtaining permission, call three
OF INFORMATION: major meat-packing houses or
                     supermarkets and request permission
                     to visit with them and look at their
                     refrigeration systems.

QUESTIONS AND   (Write a brief answer to each of the
ACTIVITIES: following questions.)

                     1. Was a written record of
                        maintenance posted near the
                        compressors?

This assignment   2. What was the interval between
sheet was provided   maintenance checks or service?
only in English
because if stu-   3. What was the general appearance of
dents are at a   the refrigeration equipment?
stage where they
have direct contact 4. What were the temperature readings
with industry, they   in the chill boxes? In the freezers?
must be able to
function reasona-   5. Describe the similarities and the
bly well in   differences that you found between
English.   the practices we discussed in class
                        and those found in the places you
                        visited.

The Problem Sheet: Description

Skilled workers routinely solve a variety of problems. Students can only be expected to develop the ability to solve those problems if they are provided with practice in successfully doing so. Thus, problem sheets are designed to provide students with the necessary practice in solving the kinds of problems encountered on the job. These range from determining the amount and/or cost of materials and supplies to human relations problems. Typical problem sheets may present a human relations problem in the form of a case study, details of a job for cost and/or quantity estimating, or some practical arithmetic problems. Regardless of the type of problem presented, the problem sheet characteristically provides all of the information needed to solve the problem.

Problem Sheet: Format

SCHOOL _____   Problem Sheet No. _____

COURSE _____   Instructor _____

Problem Sheet on (Topic)

INTRODUCTION:	Brief paragraph on the topic for the purpose of motivating the student, presenting new information, or reviewing information.
SPECIFIC INFORMATION TO SOLVE PROBLEMS:	A formula or short description of how to solve a problem.
EXAMPLE:	An example of the problem being solved.
PRACTICE PROBLEMS:	Additional problems for the students to solve.

Problem Sheet: Sample

SCHOOL C. Cohan Adult Education Center

COURSE Carpentry

PROBLEM SHEET ON BOARD MEASURE

Lumber is sold by the board foot. Each board foot is equal to a piece of lumber measuring one-inch in thickness, twelve inches or one foot wide, and is the unit of measure of all lumber.

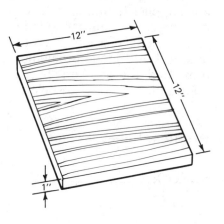

Boards less than one inch in thickness are counted the same as though they were an inch thick. Boards of more than one inch in thickness are counted at their actual size before being surfaced.

* The following method may be used for finding the number of board feet in any piece of lumber: Multiply the width in feet by the length in feet by the thickness in inches. If the width is given in inches, divide by twelve to get it into feet.

* Example: Find the number of board feet in a piece of lumber one inch thick, nine inches wide, and sixteen feet long.

Thickness		Width		Length
1″	×	9″	×	16′

$$\frac{1'' \times 9'' \times 16'}{12} = 12 \text{ Board Feet}$$

Find the number of board feet in the following:

    1 piece of 1″ × 4″ × 10′
    1 piece of 1″ × 10″ × 16′
    1 piece of 3/4″ × 6″ × 14′
    1 piece of 1 1/2″ × 6″ × 14′
    6 pieces of 2″ × 6″ × 16′

* Traducido en español.

El método siguiente puede ser usado para encontrar el número de "board feet" para cualquier pedazo de madera: Multiplique la anchura en pies por la longitud en pies por el grosor en pulgadas. Si la anchura está en pulgadas, divida por doce para convertirla a pies.

Ejemplo: Encuentre el numero de "board feet" de un pedazo de madera que tiene un grosor de una pulgada, una anchura de nueve pulgadas, y una longitud de seis pies.

> The instructor in this class found it necessary to translate only "essential information," since she had provided a good deal of oral instruction on this topic beforehand.

Problem Sheet: Sample

SCHOOL <u>American School of Beauty</u>   Mr. Mantilla

COURSE <u>Cosmetology</u>

Successful cosmetologists are as skilled in human relations as they are in the techniques of cosmetology.

Read the following true incident and complete the activities that follow.

> Mrs. Goldberg arrived on time for her appointment for a wash and cut. After nearly ten minutes passed, her cosmetologist, Fran, nodded to Mrs. Goldberg and pointed to the seat. Mrs. Goldberg assumed that it was her turn. Without any discussion, someone draped Mrs. Goldberg and shampooed her hair. Without another word, she sat and waited for fifteen minutes until Fran returned and asked her what kind of cut she wanted. Mrs. Goldberg said that she didn't know the name of the cut but could show what she wanted once the towel on her head was removed. Fran was visibly annoyed and yanked the towel from Mrs. Goldberg's head. After Mrs. Goldberg explained what kind of cut she wanted, Fran lit a cigarette and began to cut. To Mrs. Goldberg's pleasant surprise, the cut was exactly what she had wanted.
>
> Mrs. Goldberg left the shop feeling very pleased with her haircut, but determined never to return again.

1. List at least five human relations problems that occurred during this incident.
2. Describe what you would have done differently if you were the cosmetologist.

> Case studies can easily be translated into any language. Discussions that follow can also be in any necessary language(s).

The Experiment Sheet: Description

Experiment sheets are valuable supplements to other types of assignments, as they explain certain principles related to the students' work which are difficult to explain by words alone. The intention is not to have the related subjects class become an experimental laboratory, yet occasional student activities of this type, aside from having definite instructional value, add a certain amount of zest and variety to a course of study. This is especially true in the case of cooperative part-time students who seldom have the opportunity to experiment while on the job, and, unless afforded the opportunity to do so in the related class—or perhaps a regular science class—will never receive the benefits which are derived from experimenting with and verifying the basic physical laws related to their trade or occupation.

Experiment sheets may be used in any type of vocational-technical education. Although more applicable to some occupations than others, they may be used, to some extent, in all occupations in which training is offered. No extensive outlay of high-priced equipment is needed; in fact, "homemade" apparatus is preferred in most cases.

Experiment Sheet: Format

SCHOOL _____   Experiment Sheet No. _____

COURSE _____

EXPERIMENT SHEET

SUBJECT: The specific topic to be
                                discussed.

INTRODUCTION: A brief paragraph to
                                motivate the students

MATERIALS AND EQUIPMENT: Materials and equipment
                                to be used, including
                                safety equipment.

PROCEDURE: State each step in the
                                experiment clearly,
                                concisely, and in a
                                properly numbered
                                sequence. Include safety
                                precautions at the
                                appropriate steps and
                                double space between
                                steps.

CONCLUSION: Questions or discussion
                                about the experiment.

Experiment Sheet: Sample

Zapisek Vocational Center   Experiment Sheet #7

EXPERIMENT SHEET

TOPIC: Conductance

INTRODUCTION: During Experiment #6 you learned
                  something special about resistance to
                  electric current. This experiment raises a
                  question about the *flow* of electric current.

MATERIALS: 1—Low Voltage Power Supply

                  1—12 Volt lamp and lamp holder

                  2—24″ Lengths of bell wire

                  1—Glass tumbler full of drinking water

                  2—Teaspoons of salt

                  2—Needle-Nose Pliers with insulated grips

PROCEDURE: 1. Use the bell wire to connect power
                     supply to 12v lamp.

CAUTION:	USE ONLY 12 VOLT POWER SUPPLY
PREKOSION:	ITILIZÉ SELMAN DOUZ VOLT KOURAN ELEK
PRECAUCION:	USE CORRIENTE DE DOCE VOLTIOS UNICAMENTE

2. After lamp lights, cut one of the
   lengths of bell wire to break the
   circuit.

3. What would happen if you placed the
   cut ends of wire in the water?

4. Strip the cut wire ends, and, holding them with insulated pliers, place them in the water. What happened?

5. Keep the wires in the water and slowly add the salt, a little at a time. What happened?

CONCLUSION: Explain why this happened.

> Since all the Spanish- and Creole-speaking students in this vocational class are bilingual, it was not necessary to provide translations of this instruction sheet in the students' native languages. Just the same, this conscientious instructor chose to provide translations of the safety precautions—just in case.

SUGGESTIONS FOR FURTHER READING

A number of different instruction sheets were described in this chapter. Other acceptable formats for instruction sheets do exist. For other suggestions, see:

Blank, W. *Handbook for Developing Competency-based Training.* Englewood Cliffs, NJ: Prentice-Hall, 1982.
Miller, W. and Rose, H. *Instructors and Their Jobs. (3rd ed.)* Chicago: American Technical Society, 1975.

PRACTICE

Develop five different types of bilingual instruction sheets. Include a brief description of the students for whom these instruction sheets will be developed.

CHAPTER **6**

Individualized
Learning Packages

An individualized learning package may be defined as a self-contained instructional package that includes all of the components necessary to help students master specified objectives. They come in a variety of forms and are called by different names in different programs. However, whether the package is a single page or a multi-paged manual, whether it is called a learning activity package (LAP), module, learning guide, or any of the other popularly used titles, there are certain agreed-upon components of all individualized learning packages. This chapter will describe these components, present the steps involved in developing an individualized learning package, and give a number of suggestions for evaluating and modifying individualized learning packages for bilingual vocational education programs.

What is the function of individualized learning packages? To help the reader better understand the answer to this question, we will begin with a brief discussion of effective instruction in traditional vocational education programs and in competency-based vocational education programs.

TRADITIONAL VOCATIONAL EDUCATION

Individual students differ in readiness, physical coordination, emotional maturity, rate of learning, learning style, English proficiency, knowledge of U.S. educational and employment practices, and in many other ways that may influence their performance in a learning situation. Vocational-technical education instructors have long recognized the need to provide instruction designed to meet the differing needs and abilities of individual students—something which is extremely difficult to do through group methods alone. Thus, as successful teachers have discovered, instruction must be individualized, at least to some degree.

When instruction is individualized, students are typically involved in either a different learning activity or different stages of the same learning activity. Obviously, in such a setting, the instructor can personally help only a limited number of students at the same time. As a solution to this problem, instruction sheets were developed early in the history of vocational-technical education. Instruction sheets make it possible for the instructor to provide a wide variety of appropriate learning experiences simultaneously to an entire class of students with differing needs and abilities. As was discussed in Chapter 5, they serve a number of other purposes as well. Our interest here, however, is that they have been so successful in assisting instructors individualize instruction that they are now an essential part of vocational-technical education.

Individualized learning packages are a logical extension to the process of individualizing instruction. Indeed, many of them contain instruction sheets. And because they are essentially self-contained, they serve to assist the instructor to individualize instruction even more than has formerly been possible in traditional vocational education programs.

COMPETENCY-BASED VOCATIONAL EDUCATION

The general public, as well as many concerned educators, has been calling for reform in public education. This concern stems from the growing belief that far too many students graduate from secondary school programs without being prepared to function effectively in our society.

One response to this concern has been the growing emphasis on and use of competency-based instruction—an approach to education wherein instructional strategies and measurements of performance are based on predetermined competencies. Such instruction has been particularly successful in vocational-technical education, where the competencies to be taught can be readily identified, i.e., the tasks, skills, attitudes, and knowledge determined to be essential to successful employment. As in traditional vocational education programs, competencies are identified through analysis of the occupation to be taught in each of a number of different program areas. However, competency-based vocational education (CBVE) differs from traditional programs. The difference can be understood through consideration of the essential concepts of CBVE.

Essential Concepts of CBVE

1. Occupational competencies identified through research must be the foundation of the program.
2. Behavioral statements of each competency must be shared with students prior to instruction.
3. Explicit criteria for the objective assessment of each competency must be shared with students prior to instruction.
4. Development of the specified competencies using publicly stated criteria for assessment must be the major focus of the program.
5. Performance objectives representing the cognitive, psychomotor, and affective domains must be provided.
6. Instruction must be student-centered and relevant to the needs of each student.
7. Direction of learning must be provided from the identification of individual needs through assessment and feedback on performance.
8. Learning experiences must be sequential to enable the student to move from theory to practice.
9. Testing for the purpose of establishing competency must be provided for those students who wish to prove their ability to meet without instruction the performance criteria of terminal objectives.
10. Alternative learning experiences and/or recycling must be provided to assist those students having difficulty meeting performance objectives.

Notice that this list does not specify the instructional delivery system; that is, courses, seminars, modularized learning experiences, etc. are not mentioned. Thus, programs using diverse instructional delivery systems can still contain all of the essential concepts of CBVE.

The role of the teacher changes in the competency-based education setting. The teacher no longer acts primarily as a dispenser of knowledge but as a manager of learning who selects, modifies, develops, and provides a variety of instructional resources to tailor instruction to the individual needs of students. The teacher in CBVE spends much less time presenting information and much more time helping individual students master objectives. Therefore, although the essential concepts of CBVE do not specify any particular instructional delivery system, most CBVE programs find some type of individualized learning packages (modules) the most practical method of facilitating flexible adaptation of instruction to the individual needs and abilities of students.

Vocational-technical instructors simply do not have the time to provide the broad variety of individualized learning experiences, step-by-step assessment, and feedback on a one-to-one basis to the numbers of students they are expected to serve. Therefore, in practice, individualized learning packages (modules) are considered essential to most CBVE programs.

COMPONENTS OF INDIVIDUALIZED LEARNING PACKAGES

As mentioned previously, individualized learning packages contain certain common components: an introduction, objectives, (optional) pretest, learning experiences, resources, and posttest.

Introduction

This component serves to prepare students to use the module. The introduction attempts to show students the organization and structure of the module and to motivate them toward achievement of the module's objectives. Students are told how the module will serve as a means of developing a specific competency. The introduction often includes a transition from a previous module and lists any prerequisites required of the student before proceeding through the present module. A cover page and table of contents are frequently part of this component.

Pretest

The pretest determines whether students have already mastered a particular objective and provides a means of "testing out" of the module. LEP students should have the option of taking the pretest in their native language. If a pretest is used as part of the module, students should be given explicit directions for taking the pretest. Following is one example of how the directions for a pretest may be written.

DIRECTIONS FOR PRETEST

The objectives for this learning experience are listed below. If you think you can demonstrate mastery of these objectives, take the pretest. If you are not taking the pretest, continue with the learning experience.

Objectives

This component should describe the performances the students should be able to demonstrate while working through the learning package (enabling objectives) and upon completing it (terminal objective). Each objective generally specifies the desired performance, the conditions under which it is to be performed, and the criteria for evaluation. Some modules only provide a statement of the desired performance. Regardless of which form is used, the purpose of the objectives is to let the students know exactly what is expected of them. If necessary, the objectives should be provided in the students' native language(s).

Learning Experiences

This component provides activities which correspond to each enabling objective. These activities are designed to provide each student with an appropriate means of mastering module objectives. It should be emphasized that the learning experiences in a well designed individualized instructional package each contain a variety of alternative and optional learning activities to accommodate the learning needs, styles, and abilities of individual students. Learning activities can take any form; information sheets, case studies, and observing and/or interviewing successful workers are just a few examples. However, the final learning experience in most instructional packages requires students to demonstrate mastery in a real or simulated workplace situation.[1]

Resources

This component should include a listing of all learning resources to be used in the module so that they can be easily identified. Although each needed resource will also be listed at the point it is needed in the package, it is always helpful to present a complete list here so that the students can be prepared for the instruction by obtaining or locating all resources needed for completion of the package. Obviously, it would be ideal if all needed resources were contained within the package itself, but for certain resources this is neither practical nor even possible. Therefore, this component is essential to most individualized instructional packages.

Posttest

This component serves the same purpose as the pretest component. Often the pretest and posttest are identical for psychomotor performance objectives. However, in other forms of assessment it is often desirable to have a different form of the test for the posttest. In either case, the posttest provides the students with the opportunity to demonstrate mastery of the terminal performance objective. As with the pretest, LEP students should be given the opportunity to take the posttest in their native language(s).

DEVELOPING A LEARNING PACKAGE

Developing an effective individualized learning package requires the developer to complete the tasks described in the following sections.

---

[1] For a discussion of how to "bilingualize" these learning activities, see Chapter III of this handbook and Bradley, C. & Friedenberg, J. *Foundations/Strategies in Bilingual Vocational Education: A Handbook for Vocational-Technical Personnel*. Washington, D.C.: Center for Applied Linguistics, 1982. (Chapters III, V, and VI). Distributed by Harcourt Brace Jovanovich, Inc., Orlando, FL 32887

Determine the Purpose

The first step in making an individualized learning package is to determine the competency or competencies that the package will help students develop. This can be accomplished by consulting the occupational analysis, the *Dictionary of Occupational Titles*, the Vocational-Technical Education Consortium of States (V-TECS) Catalog, or a DACUM chart.[2] The essential point is that the competency or competencies must be derived from thorough research on the duties and responsibilities of workers on the job.

Determine the Objectives

The next step is to describe in specific, behavioral terms what the students should be able to perform after completing the learning package, i.e. the terminal performance objective (TPO). The TPO includes a statement of the criteria that will be used to determine whether the students have mastered the TPO, and the conditions under which the students must perform while demonstrating mastery. A well-written TPO requires thorough research of the topic. Input would include the instructor's knowledge as well as material from technical manuals and interviews with skilled workers.

When the TPO is complete, enabling objectives are written. Each enabling objective contains the same three parts as the TPO: performance, conditions, and criteria. Enabling objectives are developed by answering the question, "What are the component skills of the TPO?" For example, suppose the TPO requires the student to measure the RF output power of a CB transceiver per FCC Rules and Regulations. One obvious enabling objective is that the student should be able to identify and explain the FCC Rules and Regulations pertaining to operating a CB transceiver. Another would be the ability to measure the RF output power. Enabling objectives are, then, interim steps in the progression toward the TPO.

When the TPO and enabling objectives have been identified, the prerequisites—if any—are specified. Prerequisites are skills

[2] DACUM: DEVELOPING A CURRICULUM

The DACUM process involves bringing together a dozen or so workers from the occupation for several days. With the aid of an experienced DACUM leader, the group first identifies the broad duties and then the specific tasks performed on the job. The completed DACUM chart can then serve as a task listing. (Previously developed DACUM charts may be purchased from a central exchange).

and knowledge, not taught in the learning package, that the student must have to achieve mastery of the TPO. Most authorities suggest that prerequisites be kept to a minimum. It is considered educationally sound to sequence students through learning activities that provide the prerequisites prior to presenting the package, rather than presenting an instructional package with a dishearteningly long list of prerequisites.

Determine the Method of Assessment

After the objectives and prerequisites have been determined, the methods of assessment must be selected or developed. The logical starting point is the TPO. A clearly-stated TPO provides clear guidelines for determining the method of assessment. Appropriate assessment methods require the student to perform exactly what is called for in the TPO. For example, the TPO cited earlier called for the student to measure the RF output power of a CB transceiver per FCC rules and regulations. Assessment of this TPO *must* require the student to demonstrate the ability to measure the RF output power of a CB transceiver per FCC Rules and Regulations.

Select Appropriate Learning Experiences

In some very brief learning packages, all of the necessary information is presented in one learning experience, then the students are given the opportunity to apply the knowledge they have acquired during the learning experience. We have several difficulties with this concept. First, the skill or knowledge which will be presented in a learning package is generally too complex to be effectively included in one learning experience. If it is not, then an instruction sheet might be more appropriate than a learning package. Second, and more important, a well-designed individualized learning package provides alternative and optional learning experiences to accommodate the needs, learning styles, and abilities of individual students.

Not only must learning experiences accommodate the individual needs of students, but they must also be specially designed to build student mastery of a particular enabling objective. Mastery of all enabling objectives should enable the student to demonstrate mastery of the TPO. Therefore, this step in package development involves analyzing each enabling objective and answering the question, "What is the best way to help students master this objective?" There might well be as many different answers to this question as there are different students. And it is necessary to keep in mind that alternative and optional learning activities should be provided. However, there are practical considerations, such as time and learning resources, that necessarily limit the number of learning experiences that can be provided. It would be pointless, for example, to select learning experiences for which the required learning resources would be impractical or impossible to obtain.

The learning package developer designs as many learning experiences as necessary, and includes alternative and optional experiences, to assure that each individual student has the opportunity to progress from awareness and understanding through application and mastery of the TPO. Appropriate learning experiences require the identification of a variety of activities that enable the students to understand and practice the types of performances required in the tasks comprising the occupation. Therefore, both cognitive and practice activities should be provided.

When the instructor needs to provide the students with necessary knowledge or background information concerning the occupation or some aspect of it, the following types of learning activities could be used:

- Reading an information sheet.
- Completing an assignment sheet that directs the students' study of supplementary references (e.g., textbooks, equipment catalogs, etc.).
- Locating and examining samples (e.g., manufacturers' specifications, employment applications, news releases, employment advertisements, etc.).
- Observing an experienced worker perform a task.
- Viewing a film, filmstrip, slide/tape or videotape, or listening to an audiotape.
- Meeting with an experienced worker or other resource person to discuss concepts, obtain specific information, or examine materials or systems.
- Meeting with peers in a small-group or seminar-type situation to discuss and explore concepts, and share ideas and experiences related to the occupation.
- Solving problems designed to reinforce understanding of concepts and principles.

When the instructor needs to provide the students with practice or application of concepts, principles, and skills, any number of learning activities is possible, including the following:

- Reacting to and/or critiquing case studies or case scripts.
- Critiquing sample plans or materials.
- Planning in writing.
- Performing skills in a simulated situation (e.g., role playing).
- Developing materials (e.g., job descriptions, safety rules, employee conduct codes, etc.).
- Performing job tasks through job and operation sheets.
- Operating equipment under supervision.
- Writing reports, letters, completing employment applications, etc.
- Performing individual tasks on the job with employer supervision and approval.

Some general guidelines for selecting learning activities are:

- All learning activities should relate directly to the objective of the learning experience and to the achievement of the terminal objective of the learning package. For example, any outside readings you assign must be thoroughly checked (1) to ensure that they do, in fact, contain the information you want the student to have and (2) to enable you to assign only relevant sections of the material. Make certain that the reference is up-to-date and accurate. Looking at the title and skimming the table of contents is not enough; carefully review the material yourself.
- Material that perpetuates stereotyped sex or ethnic roles either through illustrations or written content is harmful to everyone. Such material must *not* be used. Try to locate material with examples of individuals filling nontraditional roles.
- Material that makes reference to handicapped workers is valuable (as it allows students who study from the learning packages you produce to begin to get accustomed to a world where everyone has a right to work at jobs that each can do).
- Outside references, whether required or optional, should be standard enough that they are readily available to the students.

- Use a *variety* of learning activities to suit a range of learning styles and interests and to allow for both individual and group work.
- Provide for *interaction* between the student and the teacher and with other students. Where practical, consider including interaction with employers and workers in the occupational area.
- Keep the activities *realistic*. Do *not* require the students to practice something an endless number of times if just a few performances are enough to give them the needed practice.
- Provide a system for students to evaluate themselves. Help them learn (by doing) what the successful worker does to determine that a job is well done.

The individualized learning package should be as self-contained as possible. In theory, this means that everything the students will need in order to complete the package (information sheets, self-check devices, case study problems, planning forms, checklists, etc.) is included within the package. In practice, however, this is not always possible or even desirable. The items mentioned above should always be included within the package, but there will be times when achieving the objective will require sending the students to outside sources.

Some guidelines for the selection of learning activities based on outside sources are:

- If the information can be effectively provided through an information sheet, do not require an outside reading, visit, or observation.
- Limit required outside readings to those essential to achieving the objective or those of such exceptional value that an information sheet paraphrasing the content would be a poor substitute.
- Unless they are essential to achieving the objective, activities which send the students to outside sources can be optional.
- As an instructor, you will always be involved in the final experience in order to assess the student's competency. Prior to the final experience, try to *limit* your involvement to occasions when it is *critical* for you to check the student's progress or review a product or performance. An activity involving teacher participation can be optional if it is not essential to include this type of learning activity.

List and Obtain Resources

When the learning experiences have been selected and placed in a logical sequence, it is time to make a comprehensive list of the learning resources that will be required as students work through the learning package. This is, of course, *not* the first time learning resources are considered; the developer gave serious consideration to them while selecting appropriate learning experiences. The purpose at this stage is to ensure that the list of needed resources is complete and that they are included in the package. Most developers simply begin with the first enabling objective and continue through the package until all needed learning resources have been identified. When the list is complete, the needed resources are then obtained or developed.

Fieldtest the Package

This step involves having a number of students use the package so the developer can determine whether the package needs revision and if so, where such revisions should be made. This is a crucial step in the development process. The learning package is not complete until it has been determined that it achieves the purpose for which it was designed. Regardless of how attractive or effective a learning package appears to be to the developer, or to a curriculum committee, the ultimate test is how it performs. The developer must learn what problems, if any, students encounter while attempting to complete each learning activity and, ultimately, whether the students can indeed demonstrate mastery upon completion of the package.

Feedback from the initial fieldtest provides the developer with information regarding any revision that may be required. In practice, the learning package is being fieldtested on a continuing basis as long as it is in use. That is, as experience is gained with a particular learning package, new or modified learning activities may suggest themselves. Technological advances or differing and changing needs of individual students may call for change in any part of the package. For a variety of reasons, then, the individualized learning package is never considered a completely finished product. It is continually subject to review and revision in order to maintain its ability to meet the varied learning needs and abilities of individual students as they achieve mastery of occupational competencies.

EVALUATING EXISTING INDIVIDUALIZED LEARNING PACKAGES

Regardless of how necessary and worthwhile individualized learning packages are, one instructor generally will not be able to personally develop all of the learning packages needed for a particular program. Such packages are available from a number of other sources, including other program instructors, curriculum laboratories and organizations, and commercial publishers. Unfortunately, the learning packages that are available are not uniform in quality. Some really are not individualized learning packages, regardless of what their developers may call them.

In order for vocational-technical education instructors to determine whether a package actually is an individualized learning package, guidelines for evaluating learning packages must be established. And if packages do not meet these guidelines, the packages must be modified before they are used.

This section provides guidelines for teachers to use in evaluating existing individualized learning packages for possible use or modification in a bilingual vocational education program.

The first step is to determine whether the material under consideration is actually an individualized learning package and whether the package might fit into the course.

CHECKLIST FOR EVALUATING
INDIVIDUALIZED LEARNING PACKAGES
FOR BILINGUAL VOCATIONAL INSTRUCTION

I. Is the module actually an individualized learning package? (If so, it will contain each of the following components)

	Yes	No
A. Introduction	___	___
1. Motivation	___	___
2. Directions	___	___
3. Table of Contents	___	___
4. Prerequisites	___	___
B. Pretest (optional)	___	___
C. Objectives	___	___
1. Terminal Performance	___	___
2. Enabling	___	___
D. Learning Experiences	___	___
1. Enabling	___	___
2. Terminal	___	___
E. Resources	___	___
F. Posttest	___	___

II. Will the module fit into the course?

	Yes	No
A. Is the package's TPO one of the course's TPO's?	___	___
B. Does the package take the student from awareness and understanding to application and mastery of the TPO?	___	___
C. Are the materials technically accurate?	___	___

III. Is the Module suitable for LEP Vocational Students?

If the evaluation (I and II) provides a positive response to every item on the above Checklist, the module then deserves further consideration. The next step is to evaluate the module in terms of language, bias, content, and physical appearance. To do this, use the *Checklist for Evaluating English Vocational Materials for Bilingual Vocational Instruction* given in Chapter 3 of this handbook.

PRACTICE

1. Evaluate an existing individual learning package to determine its appropriateness for your LEP students.

2. Develop an individualized learning package that is appropriate for your LEP students.

A P P E N D I X **A**

Curriculum Coordination Centers*

CCC Region	Project Director	Address	States in Coordinating Region
Northeast	Joseph Kelly, Ph.D.	Bureau of Occupational and Career Research Development 225 West State Street Trenton, NJ 08625 (609)292-5850	Connecticut, Maine, Massachusetts, New Hampshire, New Jersey, New York, Puerto Rico, Rhode Island, Vermont, Virgin Islands
Southeast	Roy Hinrichs, Ph.D.	Mississippi State University Research and Curriculum Unit Drawer DX Mississippi State, MS 39762 (601)325-2510	Alabama, Florida, Georgia, Kentucky, Mississippi, North Carolina, South Carolina, Tennessee

* Reprinted with permission from *Resources in Vocational Education*, 1982–83, *15*, 1: 181.

Region	Name	Address	States Served
East Central	Rebecca S. Douglass	Sangamon State University Building E-22 Springfield, IL 62708 (217)786-6375	Delaware, District of Columbia, Illinois, Indiana, Maryland, Michigan, Minnesota, Ohio, Pennsylvania, Virginia, West Virginia, Wisconsin
Midwest	Robert Patton	Oklahoma State Department of Vocational and Technical Education 1515 West Sixth Avenue Stillwater, OK 74074 (405)377-2000	Arkansas, Iowa, Kansas, Louisiana, Missouri, Nebraska, New Mexico, Oklahoma, Texas
Northwest	William Daniels	Airdustrial Park Building 17, LS-10 Olympia, WA 98504 (206)753-0879	Alaska, Colorado, Idaho, Montana, North Dakota, Oregon, South Dakota, Utah, Washington, Wyoming
Western	Lawrence F. H. Zane, Ph.D.	University of Hawaii Wist Hall 216 1776 University Avenue Honolulu, HI 96822 (808)948-7834	American Samoa, Arizona, California, Guam, Hawaii, Nevada, Northern Marianas, Trust Territory of the Pacific Islands

Curriculum Centers/Labs*

Name and Address of Center/Lab	Description of Activities
Vocational Curriculum Development Unit Room 802 State Office Building Montgomery, AL 36130	Produces and disseminates Vocational Technical Education Consortium of States (V-TECS) catalogs, performance-based instruction, inservice training packages. Develops performance-based instruction teacher manuals and student study guides. Material available out of state: Yes
Instructional Materials Trade & Industrial Education 202-B Skyland Boulevard Tuscaloosa, AL 35405	Produces and disseminates Vocational Technical Education Consortium of States (V-TECS) catalogs, performance-based instruction, inservice training packages. Develops performance-based instruction teacher manuals and student study guides. Material available out of state: Yes
Instructional Materials Agribusiness Education 101 Petrie Hall Auburn, AL 36849	Produces and disseminates Vocational Technical Education Consortium of States (V-TECS) catalogs, performance-based instruction, inservice training packages. Develops performance-based instruction teacher manuals and student study guides. Material available out of state: Yes
Southeast Regional Resource Center 538 Willoughby Juneau, AK 99801	Provides curriculum materials and guides, audiovisual presentations, and exemplary projects for schools. Material available out of state: Yes
Northern Institute 650 West International Airport Road Anchorage, AK 99503	Develops curriculum materials, guides, and audiovisual materials. Performs research and trains staff. Material available out of state: No
Arizona Center for Vocational Education P.O. Box 15095 Northern Arizona University Flagstaff, AZ 86011	Serves program needs (personnel, curriculum, facilities, equipment, flexibility), business and industry needs (e.g., new and existing job markets), and student needs (e.g., job interests) by providing research studies, curriculum materials, and leadership training. Material available out of state: Yes
Media Implementation Center 7701½ Scott Hamilton Drive Little Rock, AR 72209	Provides slide-tape presentations, transparencies, and filmstrips. Material available out of state: Yes

Name and Address of Center/Lab	Description of Activities
Arkansas Curriculum Dissemination Center University of Arkansas Graduate Education Building Room 115 Fayetteville, AR 72701	Acquires, classifies, and stores curriculum materials for retrieval in response to practitioner requests. Announces availability of new materials and conducts training sessions on skills needed by teachers to identify and use materials. Material available out of state: No
Vocational and Occupational Information Center for Educators (VOICE) State Department of Education 721 Capitol Mall Sacramento, CA 95814	As a computerized resource center, provides hard copy materials on request, conducts or receives searches of other data bases through NNCCVTE and the National Center for Research in Vocational Education. Material available out of state: No
Curriculum Materials Service Vocational Education Building 116 Colorado State University Fort Collins, CO 80523	Provides occupational analysis and performance objectives on a cost recovery basis. Material available out of state: Yes
Connecticut State Department of Education Division of Vocational Technical Education State Office Building P.O. Box 2219 Hartford, CT 06115	Develops curriculum materials and guides in the fields of industry, health, and service trades; adult and apprentice curriculum materials also are available. Material available out of state: Yes
Professional and Curriculum Development Unit Browne Junior High School 24th Street and Benning Road NE Washington, DC 20002	Conducts professional and staff development activities for the career development division of District of Columbia public schools. Supervises curriculum writing for vocational areas. Prints and disseminates materials developed. Disseminates NNCCVTE materials. Material available out of state: Yes
Center for Studies in Vocational Education Florida State University 600 West College Avenue Tallahassee, FL 32306	Researches and adapts materials developed by other states and organizations. Material available out of state: Yes
Vocational Curriculum Center 3417 Oakcliff Drive Atlanta, GA 30340	Provides technical assistance for development of curriculum written and audiovisual materials, duplicates and mounts slides, duplicates and edits cassette and videotape recordings, stores and disseminates composite curriculum programs, and maintains quality control for above activities. Material available out of state: No

Name and Address of Center/Lab	Description of Activities
American Association for Vocational Instructional Materials (AAVIM) 1,20 Engineering Center Athens, GA 30602	Provides resource material for agricultural education, trade and industrial education, industrial arts, and vocational technical education including manuals, teacher guides, student workbooks, audiovisual aids, transparency masters, and slide sets. Also provides a performance based teacher education program. Material available out of state: Yes
The Library Guam Community College P.O. Box 23069 Guam Main Facility Agana, GU 96921	Provides curriculum materials, curriculum guides, and audiovisual presentations and disseminates curriculum materials information. Material available out of state: No
Western Curriculum Coordination Center University of Hawaii Wist Hall 216 1776 University Avenue Honolulu, HI 96822	Collects curriculum materials and serves as a resource center for the Western states and territories. Material available out of state: Yes
Career Information Center University of Hawaii 2327 Dole Street Honolulu, HI 96822	Collects, synthesizes, develops, and distributes career information materials to teachers and counselors. Loans films, filmstrips, and other materials. Material available out of state: Yes
Idaho Curriculum Dissemination Center 216 College of Education University of Idaho Moscow, ID 83843	Collects and distributes Idaho curriculum materials. Collects and previews out-of-state materials. Serves as American Association for Vocational Instructional Materials distributor for Idaho. Material available out of state: Yes
Curriculum Publication Clearinghouse 46 Horrabin Hall Western Illinois University Macomb, IL 61455	Provides state-developed curriculum materials on a cost-recovery basis. Material available out of state: Yes
Vocational Education Services 840 State Road 46 Bypass, Room 111 Indiana University Bloomington, IN 47405	Provides loan of print and audiovisual materials for Indiana vocational educators. Modifies existing curriculum for special populations. Prints Indiana-produced curriculum materials. Consults on developing, producing, and using curriculum. Material available out of state: Yes
Iowa Vocational Curriculum Management System College of Education N008 Quad Iowa State University Ames, IA 50011	Collects, disseminates, and develops curriculum materials and conducts inservice and preservice training. Material available out of state: Yes

Name and Address of Center/Lab	Description of Activities
Kansas Vocational Curriculum Dissemination Center Pittsburg State University Pittsburg, KS 66762	Duplicates and distributes horticulture and agriculture curriculum guides. Stocks and ships materials from Mid-America Vocational Curriculum Consortium (MAVCC), American Association for Vocational Instructional Materials (AAVIM), and other instructional products for dissemination in Kansas. Material available out of state: Yes
East Central Network for Curriculum Coordination Sangamon State University, E-22 Springfield, IL 62708	Eliminates duplication of effort through exchanging curriculum information and developing products and services in a twelve-state region. Material available out of state: Yes
Illinois Vocational Curriculum Center Sangamon State University Springfield, IL 62708	Serves as a library of vocational materials and resources for free loan and use throughout Illinois and the East Central Network for Curriculum Coordination. Material available out of state: Yes
Curriculum Lab Division of Materials and Curriculum 19th Floor, Capital Plaza Tower Frankfort, KY 40601	Prepares, distributes, and utilizes curriculum materials and educational resources such as competency-based vocational education modules, V-TECS catalogs, ERIC searches, microfiche on various subjects, and other related educational materials. Material available out of state: Yes
Vocational Curriculum Development and Research Center 823 College Avenue P.O. Box 1159 Natchitoches, LA 71457	Develops, prints, and disseminates vocational-technical instructional materials; also is a member of the Mid-America Vocational Curriculum Consortium. Material available out of state: Yes
Maryland Vocational Curriculum R&D Center Industrial Education Department University of Maryland College Park, MD 20742	Provides resources and support services for vocational curriculum research and development. Includes research, collection, evaluation, modification, development, field testing, responding to requests for materials and information, and maintaining a free-loan resource collection. Material available out of state: Yes
Maryland Vocational Curriculum Product Project Western Maryland Vocational Resource Center P.O. Box 5448, McMullen Highway Cresaptown, MD 21502	Serves as a statewide center for the reproduction, production, and dissemination of vocational curriculum materials. Functions including printing, producing media, dissemination, maintaining a media loan system, and providing graphics support to curriculum development. Material available out of state: Yes

Name and Address of Center/Lab	Description of Activities
Massachusetts Vocational Curriculum Center Minuteman Regional Vocational-Technical School 758 Marrett Road Lexington, MA 02173	Collects and disseminates vocational curriculum materials. Operates free loan of materials. Material available out of state: No
Michigan Vocational Education Resource Center 133 Erickson Hall Michigan State University East Lansing, MI 48824	Serves as a search, retrieval, and housing facility for curriculum materials for Michigan. Material available out of state: Yes
Curriculum Resource Team 100 Wills House Michigan State University East Lansing, MI 48824	Produces curriculum guides as specified by, and at the request of, the Michigan Department of Education, Vocational-Technical Education Service. Format and processes are determined by the Michigan Curriculum Management System. Assists in dissemination activities. Material available out of state: Yes
Minnesota Curriculum Services Center 3554 White Bear Avenue White Bear Lake, MN 55110	Loans materials from the resource library, disseminates materials on free and cost-recovery basis. Develops program area task lists, student performance objectives, competency records, and instructional resource listings. Material available out of state: Yes, cost-recovery items; only state-developed items are available for loan out of state.
Research and Curriculum Unit Drawer DX Mississippi State, MS 39762	Provides teacher curriculum guides and resource units. Material available out of state: Yes
Instructional Materials Laboratory 10 Industrial Education Building University of Missouri-Columbia Columbia, MO 65211	Produces and distributes competency-based instructional materials and teaching aids in nine areas; agriculture, business and office education, home economics, distributive education, cooperative education, industrial education, industrial arts, sex equity, and special needs. Material available out of state: Yes
Nebraska Vocational Curriculum Resource Center Kearney State College, West Campus Kearney, NE 68847	Collects and disseminates vocational curriculum materials. Material available out of state: Yes

Name and Address of Center/Lab	Description of Activities
Learning Resource Center Keene State College Keene, NH 03431	Serves as a statewide center for the distribution and dissemination of vocational and instructional materials including those for special needs students. Services include research, teacher training, technical assistance, and information services in all vocational education areas. Material available out of state: No
Vocational Research Curriculum Office Keene State College Keene, NH 03431	Disseminates curriculum materials to new and returning vocational teachers within the state. Provides on-site technical assistance. Conducts sequence of workshops, short- and long-term, in all vocational education strategies. Material available out of state: No
New Jersey Vocational-Technical Curriculum Laboratory Kilmer Rutgers University New Brunswick, NJ 08403	Provides needs assessment, curriculum development, publication, dissemination, technical assistance, and information services for all vocational and career education subjects. Material available out of state: Yes
Sex Equity Dissemination Center University of New Mexico 3010 Mesa Vista Albuquerque, NM 87131	Disseminates only equal opportunity vocational curriculum materials. Materials available out of state: No
Vocational Curriculum Material Dissemination Center Eastern New Mexico University Portales, NM 88130	Disseminates curriculum materials for trade and industrial education, office education, distributive education, health occupations education, agriculture, and industrial arts. Material available out of state: No
Instructional Materials Service New York State College of Agriculture and Life Sciences Cornell University, Department of Education 3 Stone Hall Ithaca, NY 14853	Develops and disseminates materials and provides inservice activities related to agriculture. Material available out of state: Yes
Curriculum Field Office Oneida-Madison Board of Cooperative Educational Services (BOCES) Box 70, Middle Settlement Road New Hartford, NY 13413	Disseminates Vocational-Technical Education Consortium of States (V-TECS) and Instructional Support System for Occupational Education (ISSOE) materials. Material available out of state: Yes

Name and Address of Center/Lab	Description of Activities
South Central Curriculum Network (SCCN) Division of Vocational Education North Carolina Department of Public Instruction Raleigh, NC 27611	Provides technical assistance in and coordination of vocational education activities through this office or the chief consultant of the respective program areas in vocational education. Serves as a source of information and curriculum materials for vocational education to secondary teachers and administrators in the state. Acquires materials from each of the eight regional centers. These materials are not available from the centers out of state; however, materials can be copied. Material available out of state: No
Region 1 Education Center P.O. Box 1028 Williamston, NC 27892	Serves as a source of information and curriculum materials for vocational education to secondary teachers and administrators in the region. Material available out of state: No
Region 2 Education Center 612 College Street, Room 200 Jacksonville, NC 28540	Serves as a source of information and curriculum materials for vocational education to secondary teachers and administrators in the region. Material available out of state: No
Region 3 Education Center P.O. Box 549 Knightdale, NC 27545	Serves as a source of information and curriculum materials for vocational education to secondary teachers and administrators in the region. Material available out of state: No
Region 4 Education Center P.O. Box 786 Carthage, NC 28327	Serves as a source of information and curriculum materials for vocational education to secondary teachers and administrators in the region. Material available out of state: No
Region 5 Education Center P.O. Box 21889 Greensboro, NC 27420	Serves as a source of information and curriculum materials for vocational education to secondary teachers and administrators in the region. Material available out of state: No
Region 6 Education Center P.O. Box 1397 Gastonia, NC 28052	Serves as a source of information and curriculum materials for vocational education to secondary teachers and administrators in the region. Material available out of state: No

Name and Address of Center/Lab	Description of Activities
Region 7 Education Center 303 East Street North Willkesboro, NC 28659	Serves as a source of information and curriculum materials for vocational education to secondary teachers and administrators in the region. Material available out of state: No
Region 8 Education Center 102 Old Clyde Road Canton, NC 28716	Serves as a source of information and curriculum materials for vocational education to secondary teachers and administrators in the region. Material available out of state: No
North Dakota Vocational Curriculum Center Bismarck Junior College Bismarck, ND 58501	Disseminates state-produced curriculum materials and information. Material available out of state: Yes
Vocational Instructional Materials Lab 1885 Neil Avenue The Ohio State University Columbus, OH 43210	Develops task lists, task analyses, achievement tests, fire service, emergency medical service print and nonprint materials, law enforcement training materials, instructor and student training materials, and a subscription service for distributive education. Material available out of state: Yes
Ohio Agricultural Education Curriculum Materials Service Room 254, 2120 Fyffe Road The Ohio State University Columbus, OH 43210	Develops instructional materials for agricultural education programs at the high school and post-high school levels. Provides student and teacher reference manuals and workbooks, as well as color slide series, transparency masters, sample test items, and professional vocational education manuals. Material available out of state: Yes
Curriculum and Instructional Materials Center Oklahoma State Department of Vocational-Technical Education 1515 West Sixth Avenue Stillwater, OK 74074	Produces several kinds of instructional materials: core curriculum, videotapes, slide-tapes, competency profiles, and learning activity packets. Provides free loan films to Oklahoma vocational teachers, technical assistance, and reference materials in the resource center to vocational teachers. Material available out of state: Yes
Vocational Education Information Network (VEIN) Pennsylvania Department of Education SLMERS Division, Eleventh Floor 333 Market Street P.O. Box 911 Harrisburg, PA 17108	Acquires, classifies, and stores curriculum materials for retrieval in response to practitioner requests; announces availability of new materials. Material available out of state: No

Name and Address of Center/Lab	Description of Activities
Research Coordinating Unit Vocational and Technical Education Program P.O. Box 759 Hato Rey, PR 00919	Develops curriculum materials such as guides, manuals, and modules; performs research and trains staff. Material available out of state: Yes
Curriculum Resource Center Rhode Island College Department of Industrial Technology Providence, RI 02908	Inventories curriculum products. Material available out of state: No
Center for Economic Development Rhode Island College Providence, RI 02908	Disseminates consumer economics information. Conducts career development workshops for local school districts to show how to integrate elements into the curriculum. Material available out of state: No
Home Economics Education Resource Center Quinn Hall University of Rhode Island Kingston, RI 02881	Disseminates home economics education materials. Material available out of state: No
Vocational Instructional Services P.O. Box 182 Texas A&M University College Station, TX 77843	Provides instructor's guides, student materials, audiovisual materials in production agriculture, co-op agriculture, agriculture special needs, and industrial laboratory programs. Develops complimentary materials for all trades. Material available out of state: Yes
ERIC Resource Center State Department of Education Montpelier, VT 05602	Provides educational materials for kindergarten through postsecondary levels. Material available out of state: No
Vocational Education Curriculum Center Virginia Commonwealth University 620 North Lombardy Street Richmond, VA 23284	Prepares curriculum materials for agricultural education, business education, distributive education, health occupations education, home economics education, industrial arts education, trade and industrial education, special programs, and certain across-the-board materials. Material available out of state: Yes
Curriculum Development and Resource Center Multi-Purpose Building First Avenue, Estate Thomas St. Thomas, VI 00801	Not fully in operation at this time. The center soon will be relocated to a more centralized site. Material available out of state: No
Northwestern Curriculum Management Center Building 17 Airdustrial Park Olympia, WA 98504	Plans for cooperation in the development, field testing, and implementation of instructional materials and strategies. Material available out of state: Yes

Name and Address of Center/Lab	Description of Activities
Vocational Curriculum Development Section Office of Vocational Education Ninth Floor Rutledge Building Columbia, SC 29201	Provides student and teacher manuals, curriculum guides, filmstrips, audiotapes, and student modules. Material available out of state: No
State of Tennessee Department of Education Division of Vocational-Technical Education 205 Cordell Hull Building Nashville, TN 37219	Acquires and adapts programs from other states, conducts some needs assessment. Disseminates curriculum materials at workshops and conferences. Provides training programs in local school systems. Material available out of state: Yes
Center for Occupational Curriculum Development P.O. Box 7218 The University of Texas at Austin Austin, TX 78712	Provides instructional materials such as teacher's guides, student materials, core curriculum, individualized instructional publications and audiovisual materials. Material available out of state: Yes
Home Economics Instructional Materials Center Texas Tech University, Box 4067 Lubbock, TX 79409	Provides instructor's guides, student materials, and courses of study in consumer and homemaking education and occupational home economics. Material available out of state: Yes
West Virginia Vocational Curriculum Lab Cedar Lakes Conference Center Ripley, WV 25271	Develops competency-based curriculum. Material available out of state: Yes
Wisconsin Board of Vocational Technical, and Adult Education 4802 Sheboygan Avenue P.O. Box 7874 Madison, WI 53707	Develops and produces curriculum through project efforts with local VTAE districts and teacher education centers. Collects and disseminates secondary and postsecondary curriculum materials to local curriculum specialists and teachers through the curriculum loan library. Material available out of state: Yes
Wisconsin Vocational Studies Center 964 Education-Science Building 1025 West Johnson Street Madison, WI 53706	Develops, produces, and disseminates K-12 and postsecondary curriculum (hard copy and multimedia materials for loan free in-state, cost-recovery out of state). Provides inservice teacher training and workshops for business-industry-labor. Material available out of state: Yes
Occupational Curriculum Laboratory East Texas State University Commerce, TX 75428	Provides self-contained instructional materials for teachers and students in office occupations and trade and industrial special needs (both disadvantaged and handicapped). Material available out of state: Yes

APPENDIX **B**

Selected Visual Aids*

Visual aids are extremely useful for LEP vocational students because they can help clarify instruction with minimal use of words. Photographs serve a multitude of purposes. Illustrated safety signs help remind LEP students of hazards. Wall charts, posters, and illustrations help clarify the names of tools, equipment, and materials. Slide, filmstrip, and film presentations can demonstrate tasks and procedures even if the words involved are hard to comprehend. Other forms of visual aids include models and actual objects. Such aids are useful for all students, but particularly useful for LEP students who are new to this country or who have limited experience in the trade area.

A wide variety of visual aids is commercially available. However, instructors of LEP students often find it necessary or desirable to develop their own. This Appendix includes information useful for instructors who want to make their own.

PHOTOGRAPHY

Photo Equipment
110 or 126 cameras, 35mm cameras
Tripod
135mm, 28mm lenses
Copy stand and lights
Flash attachment
Light table
Slide duplicator
Slide camera

---

* Adapted by permission of Jo Palchinsky and Mykle Mettee, FIU Media Services, Florida International University, Miami, Florida.

USE OF THE 35mm CAMERAS: To produce slides and photographs either in B&W or color.

1. Load the film in the camera.
2. Set the shutter speed dial.
3. Set the ASA dial.
4. Turn the built-in light meter "on."
5. Look through the view finder to:
6. Line up the image,
7. Focus the image with the focus ring,
8. Read the light meter and set the aperture.
9. Shoot the picture by pressing the shutter release button.
10. Advance the film to the next frame.
11. Repeat processes 5–10 to complete roll of film.
    WARNING: When nearing end of roll, never force the film advance lever.
12. When end of roll is reached, press the rewind button on the bottom of the camera and wind the film back into the cassette *BEFORE OPENING THE CAMERA.*

USE OF THE COPY STAND

1. Use to make slides from books, magazines, artwork, 3-D objects, title cards, etc.
2. Mount camera on bar with bolt to bottom of camera.
3. Aim lights at 45° angle whenever possible.
4. Use non-glare glass on books and other glossy surfaces.
5. Use the wide angle lens for most work; add the close-up lenses for artwork or pictures smaller than 6 inches.
6. Keep all copy work on the horizontal format.
7. Use paper frames or masks to block out unwanted areas from slides or photos, or mask finished slide with photographer's tape.

USE OF THE KODAK EKTAGRAPHIC SLIDE MAKER

1. For flat work or 3-D objects in a 3 inch square or 8 inch square format.
2. Use 110 or 126 film and flash cartridge.
3. Load camera and attach flash cube.
4. Attach camera to desired copy stand; lay stand over artwork.
5. Say, 'cheese,' and snap the picture.

USE OF THE REPRONAR SLIDE DUPLICATOR

1. May also be used to convert color slides to color or B&W photos, 16mm or 35mm movie frames to color slides, film loops or film strips to color slides or photos.
2. Use film for duplicating.
3. Load film as for any 35mm camera. Set ASA dial on top of camera.
4. Set film dial located on left side of camera stand. Setting depends on type of film used.
5. Set f stop dial on the f-stop indicated on the left side indicator.
6. Decide on the size of the copied slide: 1/2, 1/4, twice as large, etc.
7. Place slide on stage with emulsion side DOWN.
8. View and focus the image through the viewfinder by pressing the "view" button on the base of the camera stand.
9. Press the "flash" button on the base.
10. Press the cable release to expose the slide. Advance film and repeat steps for the next slide.

GENERAL HINTS FOR BETTER PHOTOGRAPHY AND CAMERA CARE

1. Never force the film advance lever, especially if you are close to the last frame on the roll of film.
2. Never open a camera with film in it.
3. The lens is the most delicate (and expensive) part of your camera; therefore, don't touch it with your fingers or set the camera down on the lens. Keep a lens cover on when camera is not in use. Clean the lens with special lens tissue. Never use tissue or cloth, as it will scratch the lens.
4. Keep cameras in a cool, dry, dust-free place as much as possible.
5. Store film in the freezer or refrigerator; develop it promptly after use.

SLIDE PRESENTATIONS

. . .can be fun and easy. Since the presentation you make yourself can be exactly suited to your needs, you may be better prepared to make an instructional visual presentation than you realize. You know the subject and the problem areas, so now you are just using a new tool to do the familiar job of communicating information. The following provides a step-by-step guide that will help you make an effective slide presentation.

1. *Start with an idea or objective:* An idea may indicate an area of interest you have.
2. *Develop your objectives:* Define your objectives in a single sentence: "After viewing the slide presentation, I want the learner to. . ."
3. *Analyze your audience, the learner:* Remember that your group may be multicultural and multilingual.
4. *Collect and organize materials:* Research swipe files, libraries, museums, newspapers, and have idea-swapping sessions.
5. *Prepare the content outline:* This consists of the basic topics which support your objectives and facts that explain each topic.
6. *Develop the storyboard:* Use the "picture box" area for a rough sketch, snapshot, clipping, or some other representation of the slide you plan to use.
7. *Develop the script:* As you write, "think pictures." Try to use words, phrases, ideas that suggest visuals. Write it as *you* would say it. Be sure your narration relates closely to the visual so as to reinforce it, or the narration will interfere with or inhibit learning.
8. *Record your sound tracks:* Plan to do your recording only after you have finished editing your slides and you have completed your script. Arrange to do your recording in an acoustically treated sound-proof room. . .if possible, in a room with carpeting and cloth drapes. Avoid squeaky chairs and rattling papers. The only equipment you will need is a tape recorder, but a watch with a second hand can be very helpful. Remember that you can make a sound track in each appropriate language.
9. *Synchronizing your sound and visuals:* After your recording has been finished, you might wish to synchronize your sound to the visuals (in order for a slide change to take place at a prescribed spot on the tape recording). The second method is to record an inaudible controlled tone or signal on a second track with an electric audio "sync" generator. A sync recorder must be used to record the presentation.

Now, after you have completed the entire program, play it through to check for problems. Then, sit back and enjoy the presentation. . .because you've done it!

STORYBOARD—AN ILLUSTRATED SCRIPT

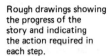

Rough drawings showing the progress of the story and indicating the action required in each step.

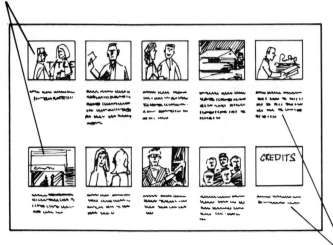

Notes of the sound effects, dialogue narration, or music to be used.

PURPOSES:
- Encourages visualization of action difficult to verbalize
- Can be used as a shooting script
- Saves time and film
- Helps determine how to set up camera when shooting begins
- May simplify editing

SUPER 8MM FILMS

FILM PRESENTS INFORMATION THAT:
- Involves motion
- Describes processes
- Teaches a skill
- Affects an attitude through individual study, group viewing, or by means of television

PLAN AHEAD:
- Clarify ideas and limit the topic
- State the objective
- Consider the audience
- Prepare a content outline
- Reevaluate (consider whether film is the best medium for accomplishing the purpose and handling the content)
- Decide if your film will be a *complete production* or a *single concept*
- Sketch a storyboard
- Prepare a scene-by-scene script
- Consider the specifications necessary
- Select other people to assist if necessary

KNOW YOUR CAMERA

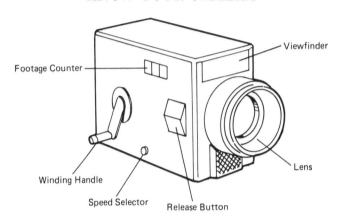

PRODUCTION STEPS:
- Filming scenes, utilizing a variety of techniques
- Processing film
- Editing
- Preparing titles and/or adding sound
- Preparing to use the film

REVIEW LITERATURE ON FILMMAKING BEFORE PRODUCTION:

"8mm Motion Pictures in Education: Incipient Innovation." Louis Forsdale, *Innovation in Education*, 1964, pp. 203–229.

The Five C's of Cinematography. Joseph V. Mascelli, Cine/Graphic Publications, 1965.
Planning and Producing Audiovisual Materials. Jerrod E. Kemp, Chandler Publishing Co, 1980, pp. 222–260.
Practical Guide to Classroom Media. Delores and David Linton, Pflaum/Standard Publishing, 1971, pp. 83–103.

BULLETIN BOARDS

FUNCTIONS:
- To stimulate student interest
- To encourage student participation
- To facilitate study of single-copy materials
- To save time
- To provide a review
- To help students learn how to communicate ideas visually

PLANNING:
- Start with an *idea* (rather than with a picture)
- Select pictures and other materials to fit your theme
- Arrange the layout (make several sketches, then select the best layout)

REMEMBER:
- "Heavier" objects or pictures belong at the bottom of the exhibit
- Informal arrangement is often the best
- Use few sizes and styles for caption backgrounds
- Limit number of letter sizes and styles
- Beware of scrappiness or clutter

OTHER BULLETIN BOARD SPACE:
- Easel-type boards
- Corrugated paper
- Room dividers
- Temporary bulletin boards of Celotex or wood-fiber panel set on chalk tray or hung from map rail
- Pegboard

POSTERS

PROCEDURE

1. Make a rough drawing on any size paper. This is for planning the positions and proportions of the words and individual letters.
2. Determine the size of cardboard desired and cut to size.
3. Start blocking areas for letters; determine margins.
4. Measure and pencil in letters.
5. Choose colors and style of lettering. Use 2 or 3 dominant colors. Too many colors cause visual confusion.

POINTS TO REMEMBER

1. Simplicity is always the best determining factor.
2. The poster should have only one dominant feature, whether it's a word, phrase, or picture. All other information should be subordinate.
3. NO CHEATING! Layout in pencil first is essential.
4. Remember that the poster has to attract before it will be read!
5. Remember to make posters in all appropriate languages.

OVERHEAD PROJECTIONS

THERMOFAX TRANSPARENCIES

The overhead transparency master should be prepared on white pliable paper within an area not to exceed 7 1/2″ × 9 1/2″. The master to be copied must be compatible with the infrared process. Compatible materials include *black* printer's ink, graphite pencil, black carbon content typewriter ribbon, India ink, and Xerox. Do not attempt to use regular ballpoint pens or colored printer's ink unless they are specifically labeled as "reproduceable."

FOUR EASY STEPS IN MAKING TRANSPARENCIES

1. Remove sheet of transparency film and position it over the original with the notch in the upper right hand corner.
2. Set the thermal copier exposure dial. A general rule of thumb is to start by setting the dial in the 11:00 position.

3. Feed the assembly, film side up, into the thermal copy machine, being careful to stay within the guides.
4. Separate the film from the original with a gentle peeling motion. The transparency is now ready for projection.

FAINT IMAGE: If your image is faint, decrease the machine speed, allowing more exposure time by moving the dial to the left of the 11:00 position.

HEAVY IMAGE: If your image is too dark or heavy, increase the machine speed, providing less exposure time by moving the dial to the right of the 11:00 position.

NO IMAGE: If no image appears, check the "four steps" procedure. Be sure the notch is in the upper right-hand corner.

YOU CAN WRITE ON THE TRANSPARENCY WITH THE FOLLOWING AFTER IT IS FINISHED:

> Grease pencil
> Colored pencil
> Felt-tip pen
> Drawing pen
> Brush
> Lettering device
> Pressure-sensitive materials

DIAZO TRANSPARENCIES

Diazo film is used to make brilliantly colored overhead transparencies. Light-sensitive paper is used, and the film must be developed in an alkaline medium, usually using ammonia fumes.

MATERIALS NEEDED:

1. Translucent pliable paper
2. Light-blocking materials
3. Diazo equipment

STEPS IN PREPARING A MASTER:

1. Plan your artwork in a 9 1/2" × 7 1/2" area.
2. Prepare one master for each color desired on translucent, pliable paper.

3. For illustrations, use India ink.
4. For lettering use:
   a. Primary typewriter
   b. Presstype
   c. India ink
5. For solid areas, use opaque paper shapes cut out and glued into place.

MAKING THE DIAZO:

1. Select desired color film.
2. Lay film on tray with notch on upper right hand corner.
3. Place master face down on film.
4. Set timer according to package directions.
5. Set dial to expose film.
6. When light shuts off, remove film (holding by corners only) and develop in ammonia fumes.
7. Tape main copy to back of frame (if working with overlays, hinge them to the front side of frame).

COLOR LIFTING

MATERIALS

Clear contact paper or laminating film and dry mount press or laminating machine, water, detergent, sponge.

PROCESS

Begin with laminated clay-base paper illustration from magazine. Immerse the laminated picture completely in water, preferably warm, with liquid detergent added. Leave it in the water until the paper begins to separate from plastic. Then, gently peel off all paper. Remove the excess clay from the adhesive side by rubbing under water with a soft sponge. After drying, you can protect the back side of the transparency by spraying with plastic spray or sandwiching with another piece of clear plastic. Frame transparency.

GRAPHICS

LETTERING:

DEFINITIONS

Gothic   Letters composed of uniform-width elements. Also
             known as sans-serif.
Roman   Letters composed of thick and thin elements. Also
             known as serif.
Italics   Letters, Gothic or Roman, created on a slant of 10
             degrees or more. Sometimes known as "script."
Point   Printer's unit for measuring type. Example: 36 pt. =
             1/2 inch.
Sans-serif   Refers to all alphabets without serifs. These alphabets
             are also known as Gothic, manuscripts, or Grotesque.

MECHANICAL LETTERING

1. Leroy templates
2. Wrico stencils/precut stencils
3. Stick-on adhesive letters
4. Rub-on (presstype)
5. Primary typewriter
6. Varifont type letter

HAND LETTERING METHODS

1. Speedball pens
2. Steel brush
3. Lettering brush with poster paint
4. Magic markers
5. Project and trace

DRY TRANSFER LETTERING

Rub-on or pressure-sensitive lettering is available in a wide variety of styles and sizes.

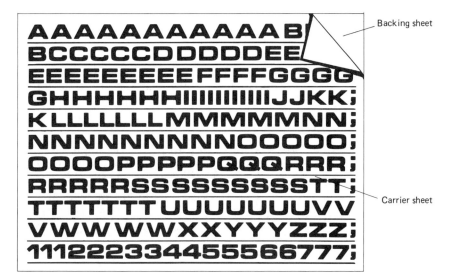

PROCEDURE:

1. Draw a LIGHT pencil guideline.
2. Remove backing sheet and place the sheet of lettering on your work, aligning the guideline and underline.
3. Rub the letter down carefully using a rounded instrument such as the cap on a BIC pen.
4. The letter is completely adhered when it has changed color, from black to gray.
5. Be careful not to break the letters by rubbing too hard or with too sharp an instrument.
6. Burnish the letters down by placing the backing sheet over them and rubbing evenly with the instrument.

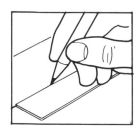

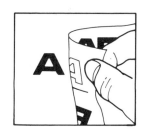

DRY MOUNTING

A. Dry mounting is a process whereby one can mount prints, maps, and other materials without the use of messy paste, glue, or cement.
B. The advantages of the dry mounting process are: Speed—it is the fastest known method; safety—no danger of paste or glue fading material; and versatility—it is permanent for silks, documents, but *NOT* parchment or thermal copies!
C. Materials and equipment: dry mount press or regular hand iron; tacking iron if available; dry mount tissue (MT-5); poster or railroad board; picture or print; razor blade or x-acto knife; metal-edged ruler.
D. Process: Preheat press or hand iron to 225°F. Preheat tacking iron medium to high. Preheat print for one minute to dry out possible moisture. Then, preheat poster board 2 to 8 minutes. Tack MT-5 to back center of print, using tip of iron at 45° angle. Trim picture and MT-5 at same time. Tack picture to poster board. Place between fold of brown paper in press 2 to 5 minutes.

LAMINATION

A. Laminating is a procedure whereby one seals a plastic film to a print or mounted picture.
B. Advantage of laminating:
    1. Waterproof—after taping
    2. No permanent smudge marks or fingerprints
    3. Allows use of felt tip pens for writing
    4. Enriches color tone of picture
    5. Longevity—lifetime permanency
C. Materials needed for lamination using dry mount press:
    1. Artwork
    2. Butcher paper, ruler, and razor blade
D. Steps in laminating with dry mount press:
    1. Preheat press to 270–300 degrees F.
  * 2. Preheat material approximately 1–5 minutes.

* If picture has not been dry mounted within last 3 hours, pre-heat at 225 degrees for 2–5 minutes.

3. Cover artwork with film—dull side next to picture, shiny side out.
4. Smooth film with side of hand.
5. Place film and material inside butcher paper.
6. Place paper into press; lock the lid.
7. Wait 2–8 minutes
8. Remove paper from press.
9. If bubbles or blisters appear, allow additional press time.

E. Laminating with contact paper:
1. Slowly separate the contact paper from its backing.
2. Place the contact paper over the picture, being careful to avoid wrinkles.
3. Press contact paper with a hard smooth object to eliminate all air bubbles.
4. Cut the laminated picture to the desired size.

F. Laminating machine
1. Preheat machine.
2. Cut artwork to fit size of machine.
3. When "ready" light appears, line up artwork.
4. Press "run" button.
5. Feed artwork in carefully.
6. Wait until complete artwork appears out back of machine.
7. Stop machine.
8. Tear off.

PAPER CUTTING TECHNIQUES

The common paper cutter is one of the most misused pieces of equipment in the school. Most teachers have not taken the time to become familiar with its correct operation. The following suggestions are offered as guides to more effective use of the cutter.

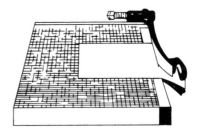

1. *MAKE USE OF THE GRIDS ON THE BASE BOARD:*
   The most accurate cut can be obtained by lining the material along the grid line. Too many people depend on the ruler along

the top. Use the ruler only to find the desired grid for the measurement of the illustration.

2. *WHEN CUTTING, PULL THE HANDLE INWARD AND DOWNWARD IN ONE MOTION:*
   To get a clean cut, be sure to hold the handle in close to the body as you draw the handle down. Apply pressure to get the material along the base board by spreading your fingers across the material as close to the cutting edge as possible.

3. *WHEN REMOVING A THIN SLICE:*
   A clean cut for a thin slice of paper can be obtained by placing a piece of heavy poster board over the material and cutting inward and downward through the board and the material. The board acts as a source of pressure to help secure a thin cut.

4. *SQUARING MATERIALS:*
   To square any material, work counter-clockwise, using the grids. Select one side, and cut a thin section off. Work counter-clockwise until all four sides have been cut.

5. *POINTS TO REMEMBER:*
   A. Use the grids on the base board—*not* the ruler.
   B. Always draw the blade inward and downward when cutting an illustration.
   C. Place extra poster board over illustration to secure a clean cut on a thin slice.
   D. Work counter-clockwise to square materials.

BIBLIOGRAPHY OF RESOURCES ON AUDIOVISUAL MEDIA AND TECHNOLOGY

Audio-visual equipment directory. (Revised annually.) Fairfax, VA: National Audio-Visual Association, Inc.

Ball, Howard G. "Try an audio presentation." *Audiovisual Instruction,* December 1978, p. 25.

Brown, James W. and Richard B. Lewis (eds.). *A-V instructional materials manual: A self-instructional guide to A-V laboratory experience.* (3rd ed.) New York: McGraw-Hill, 1969.

Brown, James W., Richard B. Lewis, and Fred F. Harcleroad. *A-V instruction: Materials and methods.* (3rd ed.) New York: McGraw-Hill, 1969.

Dale, Edgar. *Audio-visual methods in teaching.* (Rev. ed.) New York: Holt, Rinehart and Winston, 1954.

Erickson, Carlton W. H. and David H. Curl. *Fundamentals of teaching with audiovisual technology.* (2nd ed.) New York: Macmillan, 1972.

Facts about film. (16mm film, 13 min.) Chicago: International Film Bureau, Inc., 1963.

Facts about projection. (2nd ed.) (16mm film, 13 min.) Chicago: International Film Bureau, Inc., 1963.

Gardner, C. Hugh. "Shortcuts to better slides." *Audiovisual Instruction,* September 1978, p. 33.

Gerlach, Vernon S. and Donald P. Ely. *Teaching and media: A systematic approach.* Englewood Cliffs, NJ: Prentice-Hall, 1971.

Gropper, George L. and Zita Glasgow. *Criteria for the selection and use of visuals in instruction: A handbook.* Englewood Cliffs, NJ: Educational Technology Publications, 1971.

Isaacs, Dan Lee and Robert Glen George. *Instructional media: Selection and utilization.* Dubuque, IA: Kendall/Hunt, 1971.

Kemp, Jerrold E. *Planning and producing audiovisual materials.* (4th ed.) New York: T. Y. Crowell, 1980.

Linton, Dolores and David Linton. *Practical guide to classroom media.* Dayton, OH: Pflaum/Standard Publishing, 1971.

Media for presentations. (16mm film, 20 min.) Bloomington: Indiana University, 1978.

Minor, Ed and Harvey R. Frye. *Techniques for producing visual instructional media.* New York: McGraw-Hill, 1970.

Morrow, James and Murray Suid. *Media & kids: Real-world learning in the schools.* Rochelle Park, NJ: Hayden Book Co., 1977.

Oates, Stanton C. *Audio visual equipment self-instruction manual.* Dubuque, Ia.: William C. Brown, 1966.

Olsen, Jim. *Series 10.* (20 modules, 2" × 2" slides/cassettes.) Brea, CA: Viscom, 1979.

Ozalid Audio-Visual Department. *They see what you mean: Visual communication with the overhead projector.* (Rev. ed.) Johnson City, NY: General Aniline and Film Corp., 1961.

Pula, Fred J. *Application and operation of audiovisual equipment in education.* New York: John Wiley & Sons, 1968.

Salomon, Gavriel. *Interaction of Media: Cognition and Learning.* San Francisco: Jossey-Bass, 1979.

Self-instructional audiovisual equipment operation series. (20 titles, 2" × 2" captioned slide sets.) Kalamazoo, MI: Training Services, 1965–1972.

APPENDIX **C**

Resources for Sex Equity

Division of Adult, Vocational and Technical Education. *A guide to equity in vocational programs*. Springfield: Illinois State Office of Education, 1979. (ED 174 821)

Harland, R. *Fifty-one questions on the OCR (Office of Civil Rights) guidelines*. Columbus, OH: National Center for Research in Vocational Education. (A kit containing a handbook plus transparency and handout masters; $8.75.)

Kane, R. and P. Frazee. *Occupational choice: Do traditional and non-traditional women differ?* Arlington, VA: R. J. Associates, 1978. (ED 167 742)

Mathews, M. and S. McCune. *Try it, you'll like it: A student's introduction to nonsexist vocational education*. Washington, D.C.: National Foundation for the Improvement of Education. (Write: NFIE, 1201 16th St., N.W., Washington, D.C. 20036.)

Olivares, T. *Vocational education needs of Hispanic women*. (The minority series.) Madison, WI: State Board of Vocational-Technical and Adult Education, 1980. (ED 182 457)

Smith, A. and C. Ferris. *Pioneering programs in sex equity: A teacher's guide*. Washington, D.C.: American Vocational Association, 1980. (ED 185 423)

Stiegler, C. *How to . . . strategies for sex equity: The role of the vocational teacher*. Highland Heights, KY: Northern Kentucky University, 1980. (ED 189 459)

————. *How to . . . strategies for sex equity: The role of the counselor*. Highland Heights, KY: Northern Kentucky University, 1980. (ED 189 457)

Women on Words and Images. *Guidelines for sex-fair vocational education materials*. Princeton, NJ: Author. (Available from: NCTE, 1111 Kenyon Rd., Urbana, IL 61801).

Promoting sex equity in the classroom—a resource for teachers of vocational and technical education. (A packet of 12 modules available for $6.00 from: Iowa Department of Public Instruction, Instructional Services Section, Grimes State Office Building, Des Moines, IA 50319.)

Sex fairness in vocational education: Ready references. (A bibliography available from: National Center for Research in Vocational Education, Ohio State University, 1960 Kenny Road, Columbus, OH 43210.)

APPENDIX **D**

Word Games

The teaching of English is not the sole responsibility of the English as a second language (ESL) teacher. Experienced vocational teachers recognize the ability to communicate in English as an occupational skill, and will do all that is necessary to strengthen students' English communication skills through well-planned vocational instruction. These teachers understand that teaching vocational ESL (VESL) to LEP students is a collaborative effort between the VESL teacher and the vocational teacher. The VESL teacher provides the primary English instruction, and the vocational teacher provides opportunities for practice in a realistic setting. Word games can help both of these teachers provide pleasant reinforcement while LEP students are learning work-related English.

Some vocational educators might cringe at the suggestion that word games have a place in vocational education. However, educational games are, by definition, designed as learning experiences and are a normal part of the preparation for a number of complex occupations and professions.

Word games are used in bilingual vocational education to review vocabulary and structures (sentence patterns) in English, or as a means to develop students' reading comprehension. The objectives and the complexity of the word games selected or developed by the teacher vary with the language abilities of the students. Even crossword puzzles can be made to meet the language abilities of LEP students.

Fig. 1—Crossword Puzzle with Word List

CRUCIGRAMA

Instrucciones: Lea la lista de palabras y traduzca cada una de ellas al inglés. La palabra correcta en inglés se ajusta exactamente al numero de espacios vacíos del crucigrama. Por ejemplo, la palabra inglesa que significa *riesgo* cabe exactamente en los cuatro espacios establecidos para esa palabra.

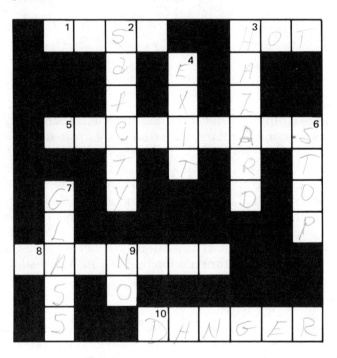

LISTA DE PALABRAS

Horizontales
1. Riesgo
3. Caliente
5. Productos Químicos
8. Admonición
10. Peligro

Verticales
2. Seguridad
3. Peligro
4. Salida
6. Para
7. Vidrio
9. No

Fig. 2—Crossword Puzzle with Phrases for Clues and Word List

ACROSS

1. Joins electrical cable and tubing to a box.
4. Fixtures installed in most rooms.
6. Permits electrical tubing to go in more than one direction.
7. Controls the flow of current.
11. Another name for a convenience outlet.

DOWN

1. A code to follow when connecting wires.
2. Another name for thinwall tubing.
3. Where appliances can be connected to the power supply.
5. A safety connection.
7. Supports electrical cable and tubing.
8. A wire that should *not* be touched.
9. When the switch is changed from the "on" position.
10. A place to make connections or attach a wiring device.

WORD LIST

Off
Color
Connector
Box
Light
Ground
EMT
Tee
Outlet
Switch
Strap
Duplex
Hot

Fig. 3—Mixed-up Words of the Trade

Here is a list of words that are used in every upholstery shop. We use these words every day, but in this list the letters of each of the words are mixed up and out of their proper positions. Can you find the words that we use every day?

1. SATCK _____
2. ROCD _____
3. RIWE _____
4. RITSP _____
5. RETDA _____
6. DOWO _____
7. WAS _____
8. LAMTEL _____
9. SALPTES _____
10. RESHAS _____
11. BEGBINW _____
12. TUTNOB _____
13. PNIGRSS _____
14. SPICL _____
15. RIPLES _____
16. MAPSCL _____
17. DEENEL _____
18. MOFA _____
19. LEUG _____
20. LINAS _____

A
B
C
D
E
F
G
H
I
J